The
RUNNER'S
RULE BOOK

.

The
RUNNER'S
RULE BOOK

EVERYTHING A RUNNER NEEDS TO KNOW
—AND THEN SOME

MARK REMY

and the Editors of **RUNNER'S WORLD**®

RODALE

ACKNOWLEDGMENTS

MANY PEOPLE HELPED make this book possible, directly or otherwise. I wish I could name them all here. Instead I'll call out a special few, including . . . Amby Burfoot, my first boss at *Runner's World*, and David Willey, my current one. My editor, Courtney Conroy, who not only tolerated my fartlek jokes but actively encouraged them. Art director Chris Rhoads and illustrator Todd Detwiler, who made this book look better than I ever imagined. Budd Coates, who has coached and cajoled me to every PR I've ever run. John "Mr. Lewis" Lewis, who once told an aimless student, "Your calling is writing." The late J.I. Rodale, who many decades ago founded a publishing company dedicated to helping people live better, healthier lives, where—years later—a weirdo runner like me could find a niche. And the entire Rodale family, who continue to make Rodale Inc. a special place to work.

I would be remiss if I didn't also thank every person who has ever raced or run alongside me. You didn't know it, but I was taking notes the whole time.

Finally, I'd like to acknowledge all of my *Runner's World* colleagues, the nicest and most passionate bunch of people you'll ever meet. Being able to work with you every day is a privilege.

Thank you all.

For Sarah, my wife and my best friend.
And for Mom and Dad.

CONTENTS

INTRODUCTION

RUNNING IS SIMPLE. This is part of its appeal. You don't need a room full of pricey equipment or a squad of team-mates in order to run. You don't need to reserve a court or phone in advance for a tee time. Running doesn't even require much skill and, in fact, is instinctual—it's as old as "fight or flight." Nothing could be easier.

Naturally, there are tons of rules.

Not for the act of running itself, of course—not for running, the verb. The only rules you need to remember for running-the-verb are these:

- Use your legs to move forward (or to avoid moving backward if you're on a treadmill).

- At some point, both feet must be airborne at the same time. (Otherwise, you're walking, shuffling, or lunging. Or skating, if you happen to be on skates.)

- Avoid running into things, such as holes, vehicles, structures, cacti, lampposts, fences, other animals, and large bodies of water.

Nail those rules, and you're in business. You are running.

No, for the purposes of this book we're talking about the rules of running, the noun. (More specifically, for those editorially inclined: the gerund.) About the act of running. About the code—largely unspoken—that governs behavior and informs decisions in situations that every runner encounters sooner or later.

We're talking about those moments of doubt that we all experience when we face a fork in the figurative road: *Do I line up for the start near the front or farther back?* (page 98) . . . *What should I say if I meet an elite runner?* (page 70) . . . *Did that driver really just cut me off, and if so, am I within my rights to flip him the bird?* (page 50) . . . And, of course, this classic . . .

What do I tell a marathoner who is lurching along at mile 20 like a zombie in search of brains? (Answer: "Lookin' good!") (page 100).

For anyone who laces up a pair of running shoes, such quandaries are inevitable.

Consider *The Runner's Rule Book* a guide for these situations—an instruction manual that, until now, has existed only in bits and pieces, here and there: a few rules in a magazine article; a few more on someone's blog; a hundred others floating in the ether, passed down from one generation of runners to another.

Understand that only some of these are rules in the classic "do this/don't do that" sense. Others are rules only in a very broad, advisory sense. And none of them are rules in the *USA Track & Field Competition Rules Book* kind of way; you won't find guidelines here on, for example, the type of pistol used to start a USATF-sanctioned road race.*

On the other hand, you won't find guidelines in the USATF rule book on passing gas during a group run (page 10). So there you go.

Regardless, I hope you find *The Runner's Rule Book* useful. Just as important, I hope you enjoy it. Because the first rule of running, as far as I'm concerned, is this:

Have fun.

—MARK REMY

---

*"Of not less than .32 caliber, with powder giving a distinct flash/smoke . . . ," in case you were wondering.

3 RULES FOR USING THE RULES

1. **Understand why these rules exist.** These rules exist to make all of our lives easier. (Yes, yours too.) To make running—and, in a sense, the world—just a little bit happier, healthier, and less irksome. For everyone.

2. **Let common sense prevail.** If ever you find yourself in a situation where obeying one of the following rules could result in mortal embarrassment; damage to property or reputation; pain, suffering, or loss of life or limb; or a flagrant disregard of community standards, by all means, *break the rule.* Use your head.

3. **When in doubt, ask yourself, *What would Pre do?*** And if you don't know who Pre is, you should probably start with Rule No. 1.10.

THE BASICS

A USEFUL GRAB BAG of tips and wisdom on everything from elite etiquette to the farmer's blow, tan lines to training plans. And the perils of asking strangers for body lube.

RULE 1.1

HAVE FUN

You THOUGHT I WAS kidding when I called this the first rule of running? No way. I'm serious about having fun.

And before you smirk and flip the page, please take this first rule to heart. It is primary and vital, and without it, no other rule in this book is worth beans. No other fact is so fundamental to running or so very easy to forget: *Done properly, running is fun.*

In fact, even when you do it improperly, running is still pretty fun (just like another animal impulse that we could mention, but won't). It is inherently, liberatingly fun. There is a fundamental joy in movement, in forward motion.

If you doubt this, just spend a few minutes watching a child or even a dog in any wide, open space. Their glee is instinctual and undeniable. I believe it was Aristotle who once said, "Tramps like us, baby, we were born to run." In any case, remember this one primary rule, and you're halfway there.

Running is fun. Indulge this instinct. Enjoy it. After all, there aren't many animal impulses that we can act on in public without getting arrested.

RULE 1.2

EXPAND YOUR
DEFINITION OF FUN

THIS IS A COROLLARY to Rule 1.1. As a runner, your definition of fun—which previously might have included such activities as visiting water parks, watching screwball comedies on DVD, and scrapbooking—must be . . . well, let's call it broadened.

For runners, fun might include:

- Waking up at 5:30 a.m. to run 10 miles

- Running in blistering heat

- Running in the rain

- Running in 400-meter circles

- Feeling as if your lungs are about to explode

- Paying a race director good money for the privilege of turning your own toes black and blue

- Any combination of the above

RULE 1.3

BE PATIENT

IMPATIENCE IS THE RUNNER'S single biggest bugbear. This is true for just about every aspect of running. Whether you're talking about training (trying to do too much too soon), racing (going out too fast), shoes (buying the first pair you see), or even nutrition (opting for a Pop-Tart over a bowl of steel-cut oats), expediency almost always leads to the poorer choice. So take a deep breath. Consider your options. Make smart choices.

Patience pays off.

RULE 1.4

BLACK TOENAILS
ARE BADGES OF HONOR

RUN LONG ENOUGH AND you'll wind up ruining a toenail or two. It's a cost of doing business as a runner.

Whether it's because your shoes are too big or too small or because you've just finished a run or race with lots of toe-punishing downhills or simply because the toenail gods happen to be in a foul mood, someday you will peel off your socks and see black where before there was pink.

Congratulations! These bruised (and possibly bloody) nails are tiny trophies, conferred upon you for toughing it out. They are black-and-blue badges of honor.

But that doesn't mean you have to flash those badges at everyone you meet. Rule of thumb: If you're socializing with a group that mostly or even primarily consists of other runners, wearing footwear that exposes your nasty nails is fine (unless it's a formal event).

Otherwise, keep those nails under wraps.

RULE 1.5

WATCH YOUR STEP

MOST PAEANS TO RUNNING (including, in fairness, this one) tend to speak of running in sterile, utopian terms. And why not? It's fun to wax poetic about bounding over the earth, loping down roads, and racing around bends in a world devoid of potholes, debris, and dog doo.

It is my sad duty to tell you that this fantasyland of running does not exist. (Not even, I suspect, in Fantasyland, where you'd have to dodge dropped ice cream cones and long lines for Mr. Toad's Wild Ride.) Instead, running in most parts of the real world involves a fair bit of leaping, skirting, and other evasive maneuvers.

Why? Because people toss all sorts of stuff from their cars: bottles, shoes, batteries. I once nearly tripped on a mangled racquetball racket. Not to mention the detritus that Mother Nature can strew before you, from pinecones to rocks to stuff you can't even identify. Step on any of it just the wrong way and you'll go flying.

Remember: Mighty injuries from little acorns grow . . . if those acorns are directly underfoot.

RULE 1.6A

HAVE MERCY ON THE SLOW

BE COURTEOUS WHEN RUNNING with others who are slower than you—particularly if you're running together at their invitation. To avoid subconsciously pushing the pace, make a point to remain half a step or more behind whoever is running at the front.

A civilized runner doesn't use speed as a cudgel to beat slower runners into submission.

RULE 1.6B

... EXCEPT WHEN YOU'RE RACING

DURING COMPETITION, IT'S PERFECTLY acceptable to use your speed as a cudgel to beat slower runners into submission. In fact, that's half the fun of competition. Just do it with a smile on your face.

Or at least a neutral grimace.

RULE 1.7

YOU'LL RUN FASTER WITHOUT A CHIP ON YOUR SHOULDER*

Is that guy honking at you? Did that van really just try to run you off the road? Was that carload of teenagers laughing at your reflective vest?

Maybe. Then again, maybe not.

Maybe that guy is honking at another driver. Maybe the van was trying to avoid hitting a squirrel or another pedestrian. And teenagers laugh pretty much round the clock, probably even in the shower and while they sleep.

The point is: Don't be so quick to take offense when you're on the roads or to instantly interpret every honk, look, gesture, or comment as a personal slight.

It's easy enough to get miffed under normal circumstances, but especially so when you're wearing next to nothing, heart pounding, and mixing it up with vehicles that could squash you like a bug. It's also a waste of energy—again, especially so while you're running. Because even if you're right, and that guy really is honking at you, so what? A spike in your blood pressure will serve . . . what purpose, exactly?

Let it go. Relax. You'll run better.

*Running with a chip on your foot, however, is just fine. Assuming it's an electronic timing chip.

RULE 1.8

KEEP THE JACK DANIEL'S JOKES TO YOURSELF

JACK DANIELS, PhD, IS a well-known running coach and the author of the insanely influential book *Daniels' Running Formula*. Jack Daniel's is a popular brand of sour mash whiskey.

These two facts make wisecracks awfully hard to resist. But please try. We've all heard them. Many times.

The first person to connect these two particular dots probably was the clerk who typed out young Mr. Daniels' birth certificate hours after he was born. And it wasn't all that funny even back then.

"Fartlek" jokes, however, never get old. (See page 160.)

RULE 1.9

PASS GAS, NOT JUDGMENT

Fɪʀsᴛ, ᴀ ꜰᴇᴡ ꜰᴀᴄᴛs:

- Runners tend to ingest a fair amount of healthy food—including plenty of fruits, vegetables, starches, and so forth.

- These foods produce gas in the GI tract.

- Gas in the GI tract cannot stay in the GI tract forever.

- Especially when that GI tract is being bounced and jostled.

- Like during a group run.

You see where I'm going with this.

Passing gas while running is not only excusable, it's healthy. It also happens to be inevitable. With that in mind, here are some handy guidelines.

- You may not mock another runner for having passed gas, unless he has previously mocked you for the same or unless he opens the door by mocking himself.

- If a runner has clearly taken pains to mask his flatulence, the polite thing is to pretend that nothing has happened.

- It's fun to pretend that the gas you have just expelled is helping to propel you forward, like a little booster rocket. That isn't really a guideline, though, is it? Okay, forget that I brought this one up.

- Rule of thumb for passing gas on a group run: If you're intimate enough with the other members of the group to discuss politics and religion with them, you may openly pass gas in their presence. (Credit where it's due: I believe Emily Post was the first to declare this.)

- Corollary to the above: If the group is entirely male, not only may you openly pass gas, you will be expected to, and the louder the better. The group may or may not then acknowledge the act—e.g., by hollering or high-fiving—depending on the pace.

- Running solo? Don't think twice. Just let loose.

RULE 1.10

GET TO KNOW PRE

"P RE" IS STEVE PREFONTAINE, an Oregon native and legendary middle- and long-distance track star who died in a car accident in 1975 at age 24. Apart from holding the American record, at one point, in everything from the 2,000 to the 10,000 meters on the track, Pre inspired two major motion pictures (*Prefontaine* and *Without Limits*) and had an outstanding mustache. Also, the following quote is widely attributed to Pre: "A lot of people run a race to see who is fastest. I run to see who has the most guts."

Not a bad quote to remember when things get tough.

RULE 1.11

SIGNING UP FOR A RACE EQUALS INSTANT MOTIVATION

A RACE—WEEKS OR MONTHS AWAY—is the proverbial carrot, dangled out there for you to pursue.

Even if you don't plan to really *race* your race (in the "run till you feel like puking" sense), registering for an event that is 6 or 10 or 26 weeks down the road remains the single most foolproof way to motivate yourself to get out there and run day after day.

Want an easy way to cement this commitment? Sign up for the race with a friend or a group of friends. Bingo! You've got yourself not just a goal etched on the calendar but a built-in support group to reach it.

Now all you've got to do is train.

RULE 1.12

DO NOT TEMPT FATE

THE SCENE: A RESIDENTIAL neighborhood street on a mild January morning.

The players: three middle-aged guys dressed in cotton sweats, jogging and chatting.

The audience: me and my dog, out for a walk.

So far so good, right? Except that these guys were jogging three abreast . . . an arm's length apart . . . in the dead center of the street. Oh, and they were headed straight for a steep, blind hill. Which they proceeded to run up.

I cringed, waiting for a truck to zoom over that hill and send those guys flying like three bowling pins. Didn't happen, thank goodness. But to this day I kick myself for not having spoken up, even if it would have made me sound like a scold: "Guys, that's really not safe. A car could come flying over that hill and not see you till it's too late."

I mean, I'm all for taking calculated risks when the situation calls for it. But that was just dumb.

The moral: Don't tempt fate. Keep your wits about you.

Live to run another day.

RULE 1.13

KEEP UNSOLICITED
ADVICE TO YOURSELF*

IF YOU'RE THE TYPE of person who enjoys giving others advice, whether they ask for it or not, running offers a world of opportunity.

Before races, during races, after races; on training runs; at the track; at the gym; even in online forums and blogs, you'll encounter runners who choose to do things differently than you do them. You will want to show each of these people the light. Resist that urge.

Unsolicited advice rarely gets a warm reception no matter how tactfully it's offered, and you must admit the possibility—as crazy as it may sound—that you do not, in fact, have all the answers. Even if you do have all the answers, the advisee may not be in the mood to hear them.

So keep your opinions to yourself unless someone asks for them. If that person at the gym really is "doing it wrong," he will figure it out soon enough. And if he doesn't, maybe he wasn't so wrong in the first place.

Exception: You see a runner putting himself or others in imminent danger; see "Do Not Tempt Fate" (left).

*By purchasing this book, you implicitly sought my advice. So I'm in the clear. Ha!

RULE 1.14

RUN AGAINST TRAFFIC

SEEMS SIMPLE ENOUGH, but how many times have you seen a runner (or runners) moving *with* the flow of traffic?

With few exceptions, this is just wrong. The law (and common sense) dictates that pedestrians—including runners—should travel facing traffic, the better to see and be seen by oncoming vehicles.

A note about those few exceptions: Usually your instincts will kick in and tell you when running with the traffic is just a bit safer than going against it, for whatever reason. Trust your instincts in these cases.

For example, there's Keystone, a relatively quiet road near our Emmaus, Pennsylvania, headquarters. Keystone is lovely but includes a treacherous, serpentine stretch that hugs a creek. This stretch of road is very narrow, and there's a certain blind curve that always inspires a swift (and morbid) calculation: Are we likelier to die if we take this curve with traffic or against it?

Usually we opt to hug the shoulder with traffic until we're well past the blind spot. And no one's gotten hit. Yet.

RULE 1.15

USE CAUTION WHEN RUNNING
THREE OR MORE ABREAST

THIS CAUTIONARY NOTE IS less about interfering with motor vehicle traffic than interfering with cyclists and other pedestrians (including fellow runners) who may be tempted to pierce you with a long-handled barbecue fork for taking up the entire width of the path or lane or whatever.

Look, it's great that you and your running buddies share this sort of camaraderie. It's awesome that you like to run side by side, so you can chat and laugh and while away the miles.

Just please be aware of your surroundings. And know that to many others, you look less like runners than like offensive linemen.

Be courteous or be sacked. Your call.

RULE 1.16

THE OPEN-ENDED QUESTION IS YOUR FRIEND

RUNNING WITH SOMEONE who's faster than you or just having a better day? Is this person oblivious to your gasping and lagging? Or—worse—aware of it, but uncaring? If so, it's time to deploy that surefire weapon of struggling runners everywhere: the open-ended question.

The idea is simple: You ask the offending speedster a question so broad, he or she could spend 10 minutes answering it. And just might! Meantime, the speedster uses precious oxygen for talking while you use it for breathing.

This is particularly useful on long climbs.

Sample open-ended questions:

- "Say, how's the job?"

- "Any vacation plans this year?"

- "Popular culture: How about it, huh?"

Related rule: If your running partner is always asking *you* open-ended questions, consider taking the pace down a notch—or finding a faster running partner.

RULE 1.17

LOOK BEFORE YOU EXPEL

THE HUMAN BODY IS an amazing machine. An amazing, disgusting machine. Particularly when you're running hard, various parts of your amazing body will produce vile substances that must be expelled from various orifices via various processes.

Most runners understand this instinctively, if not through hard experience. Most runners, therefore, are fairly forgiving if they happen to get hit with said substances. (*During a run,* that is. It is not okay to spit on a fellow runner in, say, the porta potty line or at a dinner party.)

All that said, please make a good-faith effort to ensure the area immediately around you—experts call this the Loogie Radius—is reasonably clear of others before you spit, blow, or hawk.

Speaking of which . . .

RULE 1.18

LEARN AND LOVE
THE FARMER'S BLOW

Farmer's Blow fär-mərz blō / *noun:* a process by which one clears a nostril of mucus by pinching shut the opposing nostril and exhaling forcefully [syn: Snot Rocket]

MASTERING THE FARMER'S BLOW is a must for any runner. A good Farmer's Blow is a wonder to behold, satisfying, efficient, and brilliant in its simplicity. A bad Farmer's Blow will leave you with a real mess on your hands. Literally.

Here's how to do it right.

1. Breathe in through your mouth, like you're gasping.
2. Lay a forefinger against one nostril and compress firmly.
3. Purse your lips.
4. Cock your head slightly in the direction of the open nostril and exhale forcefully through your nose.
5. Repeat with opposite nostril, if needed.

RULE 1.19

IF YOU'RE A RUNNER, YOU MUST LOVE *ONCE A RUNNER*

JOHN L. PARKER'S SEMINAL NOVEL, *Once a Runner,* about a young miler named Quenton Cassidy is, uh . . . seminal.

This means, basically, that if you are a runner, you must love *Once a Runner.* There's simply no other option. Being a runner and not gushing over *OAR* is like being an American and refusing to stand during the national anthem. No, it's worse. It's like refusing to stand during the national anthem and instead running to the nearest US flag and performing a Farmer's Blow (left) on it. It is just not acceptable.

Before it was reprinted, decades after its debut in 1978, this book sold here and there—when you could find a copy for sale—for approximately $9 jillion.

So even if you've never read it, or you tried to read it and frankly didn't care for it, you must speak of *Once a Runner* in hushed, reverential tones. Here are a few choice phrases to use when discussing the book with fellow runners.

"Classic."

"Best book about running ever written."

"The most accurate descriptions of racing I have ever read. Unbelievable."

"Yes. I totally read that book."

You want to tell the truth about *Once a Runner?* That you made it to page 39, found it dull, and gave up, opting instead to watch some TV?

Fine. Before you do, know that the federal witness protection program does not cover *OAR* disparagers. Just FYI.

RULE 1.20

YOU MAY SAFELY SKIP ICE BATHS

YOU HAVE PROBABLY READ or heard a lot about ice baths. The idea is that sitting in a tub of ice water for several minutes postrace, or post workout, speeds recovery. Many elite runners swear by the practice. Or so we're told.

Can't you imagine some running bigwigs sitting around in a bar, unwinding with a few beers after a hard day of bigwigging, and having the following conversation?

BIGWIG #1: *"Guys, I'm telling you, runners will do just about any crazy thing we tell 'em to."*

BIGWIG #2: *"You got that right. You could tell a runner to sit in a tub full of cold water for 20 minutes after a run, because it . . . oh, I don't know, because it'll help his legs be less sore . . . and he'd fall over himself on his way to the cold-water spigot."*

BIGWIG #1: *"Ha!"*

BIGWIG #3: *"Forget cold water. How about ICE water?"*

BIGWIG #2: *"Well, come on now, Bigwig 3, even runners have SOME sense."*

BIGWIG #1: *"I gotta agree, BW3. Great idea, but sitting in ice water is just too dang much."*

BIGWIG #3: *"Care to make it interesting?"*

I can't say it went down exactly like that, of course. They may have been drinking scotch instead. All I know is I've never sat in an ice bath and I don't intend to.

The drinking, however, I'm totally on board with.

RULE 1.21

KNOW YOUR PACE

I HAVE A COLLEAGUE WHO loves to innocently invite me and other hapless *Runner's World* staffers out for "easy" lunchtime runs that invariably turn into sub-7-minute-pace gasp fests. And like Charlie Brown trusting Lucy (yet again) to hold the football, hoping against hope that this time she'll stay true to her word, we always end up flat on our backs, hurting and cursing our naïveté.

It's not her fault. She's so fast that her "easy" just happens to be our "tempo pace." (Did I mention that this colleague is an Olympic Marathon Trials qualifier?) Really, we've got no one to blame but ourselves. And it does wind up being a great workout, whether we were scheduled for one or not.

But in general, please: If you ask a friend to join you for an "easy" run, it's no fair to take her out and clobber her at 10-K pace. Equally uncool: inviting someone to accompany you on a "short" run, then dragging him along on an out-and-back 12-miler. If you don't know each other well enough to understand implicitly what "easy" and "hard," "short" and "long" mean, then make it explicit: Say, "I'm going to go 4 or 5 miles at around 8:30 pace. Wanna come?" Then stick to the plan.

RULE 1.22

JOIN A LOCAL RUNNING CLUB

I AM A PROUD MEMBER of a running club called the Lehigh Valley Road Runners. (Don't ask me for proof, because I don't have any. They have never sent me a membership card.) My membership dues get me a sporadically published newsletter, a discount on some local races, and 10 percent off at the local running store. I think.

Truth is, I rarely take advantage of those perks. And even if I didn't get them at all, I'd still pony up my 20 bucks a year to be a member of the LVRR. Why? Because my running club is full of nice people doing nice things. And it makes me feel good to be a small part of that.

They sponsor a scholarship. They organize races, including a fantastic kids' series every summer. They have a potluck after their Wednesday night 5-K Summer Series races. It's good stuff.

Plus, the LVRR clubhouse down in the Parkway has a nice bathroom. That perk has come in handy more than a few times.

RULE 1.23

NEVER LEAVE A MAN BEHIND . . .

U NLESS HE INSISTS he's okay with it.

Even on group runs of just three or four people, sometimes one runner will fall off the pace and drift behind. This may happen even if no one is particularly "pushing the pace" and even if the straggler doesn't have a habit of telling knock-knock jokes (though that might increase his odds of being dropped).

This leaves the lead group with several choices.

A. Continue at their faster pace and leave the straggler to his own devices.

B. Slow down until the straggler catches up, and then either:

1. Maintain this slower pace for the duration of the run.

OR

2. Resume the previous pace, and see if the straggler can hold on.

C. Send a delegate back to assess the situation and give the straggler a chance to say "You guys go ahead."

D. Wait for a volunteer or volunteers to offer to join the straggler and finish the run with him, in effect splitting the group run into two (smaller) group runs.

(continued)

Option A should never be realistically considered. Leaving someone behind without at least acknowledging the situation just ain't right—even if he does have a horrible sense of humor.

Option B1 is nice, provided the new pace isn't painfully slow and the remainder of the run isn't too long; it is *necessary* if the straggler is the only one in the group who knows the way back.

B2 is acceptable if you know the straggler is a strong runner who likely just experienced a bad stretch and might consider a slower pace patronizing.

Options C and D are equally courteous and most likely to please the greatest number of people.

One corollary to this rule: It's fine to ask once or twice if a straggler is okay or wants you to slow down for him. Asking three or more times, however, is more likely to annoy than to help. Take the straggler at his word and run accordingly.

RULE 1.24

NEVER SLOW THE REST
OF THE GROUP DOWN . . .

U NLESS THEY INSIST they're okay with it.
This, of course, is the flip side of the previous rule, when you are the one who's straggling behind the group. If you feel safe and secure enough to run alone—assuming you know your way back—the courteous thing to do is to wave the others ahead.

You also might want to reconsider the whole knock-knock joke shtick.

RULE 1.25

LOVE YOUR TAN LINES

YOU MAY BE TEMPTED to "even out" any tan lines left from your running watch, socks, and/or ID bracelet. Don't. Those tan lines aren't something to be ashamed of. Far from it. They are hard-won emblems of accomplishment. Sport them proudly!

RULE 1.26

TRAINING PLANS MUST
GO ON THE FRIDGE

TECHNOLOGY IS A WONDERFUL thing. Many Web sites—including RunnersWorld.com, of course—offer online training logs, plan generators, and so on. You can create training programs, log your routes and mileage, and track your progress through graphs and such. Some programs let you generate pie charts, for crying out loud. Pie charts!

Still, nothing can replace the printed-out training plan stuck to the refrigerator.

This is not to say you can't or shouldn't take advantage of the online versions. You can and should. It's just that you really do owe it to yourself to have that hard copy there on the fridge. Whether it's the daily, in-your-face placement or the old-school tribute factor, there's simply no substitute for having your full 10-, 12-, or 16-week plan out there for all to see on good, old-fashioned paper. Plus, there's a singular satisfaction to be had from drawing a big fat X through the previous day's workout.

So put the plan on the fridge. Remove a child's artwork to make room, if need be. We won't judge.

RULE 1.27

ACKNOWLEDGE FELLOW RUNNERS IN PUBLIC, BUT BE COOL ABOUT IT

THIS ASSUMES, OF COURSE, that you can identify fellow runners in the first place.

How can you spot a fellow runner out of context? Lots of ways. Tan lines, for starters (page 28). Telltale wristwear. (A Timex Ironman, funky Nike watch, or chunky GPS unit is a strong clue.) Sporty sunglasses. Race tees or technical shirts. Beat-up running shoes. (They've outlived their usefulness for actual running, you know, but are great for wearing out and about.) A copy of *Runner's World* or *Running Times* tucked under an arm. And above all: a certain lean, gaunt look in the face—even if the person in question is not otherwise particularly lean or gaunt. (You know "the look" when you see it.)

Acceptable forms of acknowledgment include the following:

• Brief eye contact and subtle nod

. . . Actually, that's about it. We runners are a dignified, understated bunch. If we weren't, we'd be golfers.

Under extraordinary circumstances—e.g., if the fellow runner is wearing the T-shirt of a race that you have run—you may verbalize this fact. This is especially true at airports, for reasons that have never been made clear.

Otherwise, the nod is plenty.

RULE 1.28

ANSWER CRITICS WITH A SMILE

RUNNING IS A BEAUTIFUL—and beautifully simple—sport. It clears the mind, strengthens the heart, and burns flab. Most people get this. A few don't, and will never miss a chance to tear running down, or jab its adherents in the chest with a rhetorical finger.

Oddly enough, the most vocal of such critics are often in terrible health themselves.

"Bad for your joints," they'll jab.

"You'll get arthritis," they'll jab further.

"Running marathons?" they'll ask, jabbingly, between sips of their Big Gulp. "That'll kill ya."

Resist the temptation to confront such naysayers—despite the fact that they tend to be such easy targets. Words won't sway them. The best response to arguments like these is to continue running and loving it. Meantime, try inviting these critics to join you for a short run.

Who knows? Maybe someday they'll accept your invitation. And their own experience will be the most powerful prorunning argument of all.

RULE 1.29

KNOW WHEN ENOUGH IS ENOUGH

As WITH ANYTHING, in running there's a fine line between "avid" and "addicted." And as with other types of addictions, the same warning signs apply.

- Has running interfered with your job?

- If you're in school, has running affected your studies or your grades?

- Do you run at the expense of spending enough time with family and loved ones?

- Do you feel depressed, nervous, or irritable if you miss a run?

- Have you run while injured, rather than focusing on recovery?

In short: Do you run because you want to, or run because you *need* to?

It's a question no one else can answer for you. But first you have to have the guts to ask it.

RULE 1.30

TEAM UP FOR
EARLY-MORNING RUNS

WAKING UP FOR AN EARLY RUN can be tough. This is especially true if you're not a "morning person" and doubly especially true if it also happens to be dark, cold, windy, wet, or icy outside. Or all of the above.

Add a few margaritas the night before, and the odds of your rolling out of bed and pulling on your running shoes at 6 a.m. approach laughable.

Unless you've promised to meet someone.

If that's the case, you might shudder. You might grimace and groan. You might curse. But you'll throw back the covers, put on a pot of coffee, and get dressed. Because knowing there's someone out there, also waking up and getting dressed in the dark to run at this ungodly hour, is just enough motivation to get you moving.

And you know what? Nine times out of 10—or better—you'll be glad you did. So will your running partner.

RULE 1.31

KEEP WARNINGS SHORT
AND SWEET

ANIMALS AND BIRDS have certain calls to alert the group to potential danger, or relay other important information. Runners do, too. Or should.

The reason, of course, is that in group runs—especially largish ones—one or two runners will invariably spot dicey stuff well before anyone else can. It is their duty to communicate such diciness to the rest of the group, and to do so in a clear, blunt way.

Personally, I started my athletic life as a cyclist, so I naturally use the same kind of language in group runs that we used in group rides. For instance, "Car back!" to alert others that there is a car approaching from behind. Or "Car up!" if there's a vehicle headed toward us. Not much room for interpretation or confusion there.

Not all situations are that clear-cut. In these cases, you'll have to improvise. For instance: If your group is approaching an intersection and you spot a truck speeding along that no one else seems to see, you don't exactly have time to say, "Chaps, beware the truck proceeding eastbound on Main Street; it does not appear to be slowing, and it is unclear whether the driver is aware of our presence."

Instead, you shout, "HO-ohhh!" And the others get it.

Or, perhaps, "HEADS UP!" which I've used long enough to have gradually shortened it to a simple "Z'UP!"

Whatever works for you. The point is to keep everyone aware—and alive.

RULE 1.32

BEWARE GHOST TRAINS

EVERY SO OFTEN, as a road runner, you will find yourself crossing train tracks. Naturally, you will want to exercise caution in these moments—look to the left, to the right, and to the left again; when you're satisfied no train is coming, proceed across the tracks and on your way.

Too many runners, however, skip this protocol when they're crossing tracks that are clearly not in use (rusted, overgrown with weeds, etc.). This is a mistake, for one simple reason:

Ghost trains.

That's right, ghost trains, clattering along at breakneck speed, damned for all eternity to steam en route to who-knows-where. Probably manned by a skeleton engineer who can't be bothered to slow, let alone stop, for some mortal runner such as you.

Do we have documented cases of such ghost trains colliding with runners? No.

Here's another question: Would you like to be the first?

Me neither. This is why I always glance both ways before crossing railroad tracks. Even the "abandoned" ones.

RULE 1.33

USE YOUR HEAD WHEN YOU
STASH YOUR KEYS

I F YOU'RE LIKE ME, the vast majority of your runs begin and end at home or at the office. Every so often, though, you will drive somewhere to race or meet friends for a run. You will strip down to shorts, shirt, and shoes. You will lock your car. And then you will stare at the tangle of keys, fobs, frequent-shopper cards, bottle openers, rabbits' feet, Mini Mag-lites, and other assorted tchotchkes in your hand and wonder what the heck you should do with them.

You'll be tempted to place them atop one of your tires. Don't. That's the first place a thief will look. (If you're this person, you also "hide" your wallet in your shoe at the beach. Am I right?)

There are any number of more creative—and less thief-friendly— alternatives.

One is to remove just your car key, then stow it in the pocket of your shorts or jacket, or in a special shoelace pouch designed for that purpose.

Another method, which I've heard of but never witnessed, involves placing your keys atop the tire of someone else's car. Which I guess would work well, unless that driver leaves before you do. Yet another method is to drive a jalopy in such poor shape that no one in his right mind would ever want to steal it.

Personally, I encounter this situation whenever I meet friends for a run at the nearby Parkway. Usually, I lock up the car and take my keys with me—just for the first few minutes of the run, at which point I tuck them into the crook of a tree branch just off the path. Hasn't failed me yet.

(Hint for car thieves in eastern Pennsylvania: It's the tallish tree next to another tallish tree. With leaves.)

RULE 1.34

READ THE SPORTS
SECTION BACKWARD

IF YOU'RE LOOKING FOR articles or results on road racing or track and field, you'll find them faster if you flip through the sports section of the newspaper in reverse. This is just as true for large, nationally distributed newspapers of record as it is for your local Anytown Herald-Tribune.

For whatever reason, sports editors who happily devote scores of column inches, color photos, and charts to coverage of any of the "ball sports" or hockey, or even horse racing, carve out the smallest possible space for running—usually under the heading OTHER or IN BRIEF, presumably because the phrase OF LITTLE CONSEQUENCE takes up too much room. (The same holds true for cycling coverage, by the way, which is some consolation.)

An American could win the Boston Marathon in world-record time while juggling hamsters during a year in which Boston also happened (for the first time) to be the setting for the World Championships Marathon and also the Olympic Marathon and do back-flips across the finish line while reciting the national anthem (while the hamsters also do tiny backflips), and American newspaper sports editors would give the story two paragraphs on page C-11, under a yacht race recap.

Also, they would misspell the runner's name.

Someday, this may change. Until then, read the sports section backward.

RULE 1.35

JUST RUN AROUND THE BLOCK

O N DAYS YOU DON'T feel like running at all, tell yourself you'll just jog around the block. Then go do it. Nine times out of 10, those few minutes of movement will be enough to kick you into gear, and you'll want to keep going.

And that one time out of 10? Hey, at least you've run one block. Which is one block more than most folks will run that day.

RULE 1.36

RUNNING ON THE BEACH
IS OVERRATED

SAND. SUN. CRASHING SURF. What's not to like?

How about: a loose, shifting running surface. Driftwood and garbage. The vaguely funky smell of a Dumpster behind Red Lobster. And tiny, irritating granules in your socks and shoes, which will be there for the next 2½ months.

Not to mention the occasional sunbathing retiree with white hair and leather-brown skin, staring at you from behind BluBlocker wraparounds.

The sad truth is that running on the beach is never quite as good as you've been led to believe.

My advice? Stick to the treadmill at your hotel. Or run around town. (Even parking meters and traffic lights are better than fishy funk and BluBlockers.) Or just take a few days off from running.

Meantime, relax. Catch some rays on the beach. Maybe you'll see some poor sap out running.

RULE 1.37

RUNNING AT NIGHT
IS UNDERRATED

IF BEACH RUNNING is way less than it's cracked up to be, nighttime running is way more.

First of all, it's not that dangerous if you do it right. In fact, given the heightened sensitivity most night-runners have to potential hazards—and the reflective gear and lights they're wearing (or should be)—running at night might actually be safer than its daytime equivalent.

Plus, there's something about running through the dark, along your own narrow path of light, that makes you feel a little bit like you're gliding, whatever your speed. Which is a pretty cool feeling. There's also that peace and stillness that only comes with darkness.

Of course, this assumes that you are, in fact, wearing reflective gear and lights. (Headlamps are best, if you ask me.) And that you're not hitting the roads around 2 a.m., when all the bars close.

It also assumes that you didn't just leave one of the aforementioned bars.

RULE 1.38

RUNNING ALONE IS THE BEST;
SO IS RUNNING WITH A GROUP

MANY RUNNERS RUN ALONE, exclusively or nearly so, out of necessity. Think residents of very rural areas, or folks who work odd hours when everyone else is sleeping, or hermits in mountain cabins.

That is just fine.

Others run solo because they prefer it that way. Running gives them a chance to be alone with their thoughts, offering an oasis of peace and solitude in an otherwise hectic life.

That's fine, too.

Yet others crave the companionship and conversation of running with a group. For them, running is best as a shared experience, and running with others helps to motivate them. Maybe they run with old friends, or use running as a way to make new friends.

And that is . . . yep, you guessed it: also fine.

This is just one of the beautiful things about running—the fact that it can be equally rewarding done alone or with others, and the way that each of us is left to determine what sort of mix works best for us.

Run alone. Run with others. It's all good.

RULE 1.39

RUNNERS DO NOT SHAVE
THEIR LEGS

E XCEPTIONS TO THIS RULE:

- Most North American women

- Runners about to undergo some sort of leg surgery

- Runners who are also competitive swimmers

- Runners who are also competitive cyclists

- Runners who are also triathletes

- Runners who don't give a flip what any rule book says because they just like the way smooth legs feel, especially against cotton sheets; and anyway, what's the big deal?

RULE 1.40

GOOD DRIVERS
MAKE GOOD RUNNERS

IT'S A SAD FACT that runners and drivers are often at odds, competing for space on the road and clashing at intersections and stop signs. But oddly enough, many of the same characteristics that define a safe, skilled driver also apply to the safe, courteous runner.

- You are aware of your surroundings.

- You merge with caution.

- You make yourself visible—especially when it's dark, overcast, or rainy.

- You are patient and predictable—no sudden veering or turning or stopping or going.

Of course, the inverse is true as well. A lousy driver shares plenty of traits with a reckless runner.

- You're distracted, not focused on what you're doing.

- You take dumb chances.

- You assume everyone else sees you and knows what you're about to do.

- You're antsy and erratic—weaving around others without looking behind you, speeding through intersections despite oncoming traffic, stopping without warning.

I'd write more, but my phone is ringing and it looks like the light's about to turn green. Gotta go!

RULE 1.41

NO TWEETING, TEXTING,
OR TYPING

I T'S UNFORTUNATE THAT WE even need to address this here, but apparently we do: As this book was being edited, a jogger in the United Kingdom literally ran into a tree . . . while sending a "tweet" on his BlackBerry. He got a black eye and a bruised ego.

I know, I know. I got a good laugh out of it, too. But there's a serious lesson here.

If you want to carry a cell phone or something while you run, for emergencies, that's perfectly fine.

If you want to use that cell phone or something *while you run,* that is not.

End of lesson!

RULE 1.42

STRETCH IF YOU WANT TO

IF YOU'RE LOOKING FOR hard evidence of stretching's benefits (or lack thereof), good luck. Fact is, it just doesn't exist. And if you want to ask other runners or doctors or physical therapists or high school track coaches or the guys replacing your neighbor's roof for their opinion, go for it. Just be prepared to hear a different opinion from each one of them, delivered with exactly the same level of conviction. (The only thing most folks seem to agree on is that if you're going to stretch, do so after you run. Or at least after a warmup.)

Runner's World's advice? Save yourself a lot of grief, and follow this rule:

If stretching seems to help you run better and feel better, then stretch. If not, then don't.

RULE 1.43

REST IS TRAINING, TOO

IT MAY NOT FEEL LIKE IT, but kicking back and relaxing is part of training. Ditto for a good night's sleep. Hard running breaks muscle down; recovery is when that muscle repairs itself. The result is greater strength. Remember this if you're ever tempted to go hard on back-to-back days.

You might be able to ignore this rule for a while, but it will inevitably catch up with you. Injuries, in a sense, are the body's way of saying, "Okay, you know what? Enough is enough. Time for a little break." (For example, a "little break" in your fifth metatarsal.)

On a personal note: I've been biking or running regularly for nearly 25 years, and I can count on one hand the number of weeks I've been sidelined with any kind of overuse injury. I have a hunch this is because I was fortunate enough to be born very biomechanically efficient—my flat feet notwithstanding. But this record is due partly, I'm sure, to my habit of taking regular breaks: at least 1 day off per week; 1 easier-than-normal week per month; 1 easier-than-normal month per year.

Eventually, I think, I'll have earned an entire year to take easier than normal.

But not yet.

RULE 1.44

ONE DAY A WEEK, RUN NAKED

WHEN I WAS IN COLLEGE, before I really got into running, I was a bike racer. I trained regularly with a small group of guys, and we had a tradition called No Helmet Mondays. Which is exactly what it sounds like: Every Monday, we would meet for our ride, as usual, but sans helmets.

What a dumb move.

Still, reckless as this example is, it was fun to have a standing sort of theme 1 day each week. As runners, we don't really have much in the way of safety equipment—and if we did, I would never suggest you skip using it 1 day a week. But here's a similarly inspired idea I think you'll enjoy.

Once a week—maybe on an easy day—leave your running watch at home, head out the door, and just . . . run. While you're at it, leave your GPS at home, too, and your heart rate monitor, cell phone, MP3 player, and whatever other modern gizmo you normally carry on a run.

You'll be amazed at how liberating it can be.

And for the record: Now, when I get on a bicycle, I always wear a helmet.

RULE 1.45

BE CAREFUL WHERE AND WHOM
YOU ASK FOR LUBE

IT'S A SIMPLE QUESTION: "Do you have any body lubricant?" And asked in a specialty running store or at a race expo, it'll get you a simple yes or no answer.

Asked in other contexts, however—a drugstore, a supermarket, a singles retreat—it could yield anything from a raised eyebrow to a very unwelcome invitation.

RULE 1.46

FOR PETE'S SAKE, STAND STILL AT RED LIGHTS

Sharks die when they stop moving. Runners do not. Please keep this in mind next time you encounter a don't walk sign or a busy intersection.

There's no need to shuffle or bounce or jog in place or dance from foot to foot like you have to pee. Instead, just chill. Wait a few moments. Then resume running.

Don't worry—you will not "cool down" catastrophically in the time it takes the light to change. Your quest for fitness will not suffer a setback. Your heart will not freak out, wondering what the heck is going on.

Consider using this downtime to shut your eyes and take a few deep breaths, or look up and appreciate the sky for a bit—things you can't do while running.

Note: If a nonrunner waiting with you to cross the street is dancing from foot to foot, he or she may indeed have to pee. Give this person some room.

RULE 1.47

LET ANGRY MOTORISTS GO

T RUST ME: I UNDERSTAND the impulse to "teach a lesson" to a driver who just pulled out in front of you or turned directly in your path or otherwise behaved like a jerk while you're trying to run.

I know how much you'd love to slap the hood or trunk of that driver's car, or shout at the person behind the wheel, helpfully suggesting that he or she "learn how to drive." Or even extend a certain digit in a certain direction.

Do yourself—and, by extension, all runners—a favor and fight that impulse. Take a breath. Count to 10. Smile. Just be glad that you're happy and healthy and out for a run.

In other words: Let it go. (Unless the driver in question is a true menace, and you or someone else is in imminent danger—in which case you should do your best to get the car's plate number and alert a cop ASAP.) Your lashing out isn't likely to change the driver's behavior, and may, in fact, worsen it. For all you know, the still-seething guy may drive extra close to the next runner he sees, just to make a point. Maybe too close.

Have an urge to teach someone a lesson? Do it in a classroom, not on the roads.

RULE 1.48

NONRUNNERS DON'T CARE THAT MUCH ABOUT YOUR RUNNING

I T'S FINE TO CHAT about running with nonrunners. If they ask you about it, of course, it'd be rude not to. But for everyone's sake, know your limits.

Here are some examples of what's acceptable and what's not, when socializing with civilians.

OKAY	NOT OKAY
Mentioning your last marathon	Reciting the mile splits of your last marathon, along with your heart rate when each split was recorded, the relative humidity on race day, what you wore (and why), and exactly what happened just shy of that porta potty at mile 17
Describing the color of your favorite running shirt	Describing the color of your urine ("It's pretty dark, almost like iced tea, which means I'm dehydrated. Speaking of which, can I get you a drink?")
Quoting Sebastian Coe	Quoting Sebastian Coe, then becoming belligerent when no one recognizes the quote as being from Sebastian Coe
Showing off the weight you've lost since you started running	Showing off the toenails you've lost since you started running

RULE 1.49

THERE WILL ALWAYS BE SOMEONE SLOWER THAN YOU

M ANY WOULD-BE RUNNERS ARE deterred by the conviction that they're too slow, and the fear that if they ever enter a race, they'll surely finish last. This is nonsense.

The fact is that there is always someone slower than you. Always.

"But surely," you must be thinking, "somewhere in the world there exists a runner so very pokey that he or she is the slowest runner in the world. By definition, there can be no one slower than this poor bastard."

Well, first of all, watch the language. And second, no, this is not the case. There is someone slower than the slowest person and someone slower than *that* person.

Scientists are still trying to figure out exactly how this is possible, but that's the reality.

So if you're looking for an excuse not to run, keep looking.

RULE 1.50

THERE WILL ALSO ALWAYS
BE SOMEONE FASTER THAN YOU

SO DON'T GO GETTING COCKY.

RULE 1.51

A PR IS A PR FOREVER, BUT . . .

YOU MAY ADVERTISE A personal record (PR) time, or otherwise claim it as your own with no further explanation or context, for 2 years after setting it.

After 2 years, however, it becomes uncool to tell people, "My marathon PR is 3:12" without providing a disclaimer—e.g., "My marathon PR is 3:12, but I ran that 63 years ago."

In short: A PR has a shelf life of 2 years. After that, it's still a PR—just with an asterisk.

RULE 1.52

RUN LIKE A DOG

M Y DOG, A SHEPHERD mix named Cooper, doesn't care where we are or what time of day or night it is, or even what the weather is like. He doesn't know what his resting heart rate is and rarely bothers to wear a watch. Anytime, anyplace, for any reason, he just loves to run.

Watching Cooper run is a treat because it's an exercise in pure joy. He just switches his brain off and goes. And every time he does—every single time—his face and his body telegraph one simple message: This. Is. AWESOME. I cannot BELIEVE I get to do this! I'm runningrunningrunningrunning!

How many of us can say that?

When it comes to being better runners, we could all learn a thing or two from our dogs.

Find a squirrel to chase (even if it's a metaphorical one). When you have a chance to go off-leash, make the most of it. Notice things. Understand that it's awfully fun to run as fast as you can but that slowing to a trot has its own rewards. Stop to smell the roses and occasionally eat them. If someone asks, "Wanna go outside?" answer in the affirmative. And whatever you do, do not pee on that old guy's lawn. Because he will yell.

(continued)

THE "RUN LIKE A DOG" WORKOUT

- Warmup: Walk 8 seconds.

- Trot 4 seconds.

- Stop. Sniff.

- Sprint 7 seconds.

- Freeze.

- Walk 5 seconds in any direction but forward.

- Pause. Stare 9 seconds.

- Lunge at rabbit.

- Stop.

- Double back, walk 3 seconds.

- Urinate.

- Repeat six to eight times.

- Cooldown: Collapse on rug.

RULE 1.53

ALWAYS BE GROWING

To paraphrase ALEC BALDWIN'S character in *Glengarry Glen Ross*: A, B, G.

A, *always*. B, *be*. G, *growing*. *Always . . . be growing*.

Just be careful how you define *growth*.

The desire to do better, to improve, is natural. No one likes to feel complacent or bored or stuck in a rut. Especially when you're a runner (doubly so when you're a new runner) and "progress" can be measured so precisely and so regularly in the form of miles run, splits recorded, times clocked.

We can get into trouble, though, when we equate growth with a single superlative, such as *faster*. Not only is that counterproductive, it's a surefire route to injury or burnout or both.

Runners plateau. It's one of life's sad inevitabilities that, sooner or later, you will run as fast, or as far, as you ever will. The good news: How you respond to this is entirely up to you. You could hang up your racing flats, retire from running, and regale your friends with tales of your running past. Or you could find new ways to grow.

Instead of pushing yourself to go faster, you could slow down a bit and try going farther. Or, if you've always focused on marathons, try shorter stuff. Or trail running. Or triathlons. Or aim to run, or race, in all 50 states. Or to run a marathon with perfectly even splits, no matter what your overall time.

Maybe your challenge is simply finding the motivation to get out the door on a particularly bad day.

One of the beautiful things about running is its flexibility. There's plenty it can teach us and lots of ways it can challenge us—if we're up for it.

RULE 1.54

THE HARDEST PART
ABOUT RUNNING IN THE RAIN
IS GETTING WET

IN OTHER WORDS: Once you're soaked, you're set.

Running in the rain can be downright enjoyable, assuming you're dressed for it. (Hypothermia is a very real threat if you're wet—even if the ambient temperature isn't all that low.) After a certain point, it's not like you're going to get any wetter.

Some of my favorite runs have been done in the rain, from a light drizzle to a downpour. Showers tend to surround you with that earthy, rainy smell, which is always nice. The drops feel good on your skin. And the looks you get from nonrunners, peeking out from car windows or dashing across streets, are priceless.

That said, you are entirely within your rights to throttle any fellow runner who, in the middle of a downpour, chirps, "Oh well, the human body is two-thirds water anyway!"

RULE 1.55

IDENTIFY YOURSELF

WARREN GREENE, BRAND EDITOR of *Runner's World,* who happens to be a good friend of mine, is a very healthy guy. A lifelong runner and veteran of several marathons, Warren had no reason to expect that a 6-mile run he took back in August 2005 would be remarkable in any way. He set off from his Allentown, Pennsylvania, apartment and headed west toward Trexler Park, no problem. The first several miles rolled by, no problem. He looped through Cedar Beach Park on his way home, no problem.

Then an aneurysm popped in his brain.

Big problem.

Of course, Warren didn't know at the time that it was an aneurysm. He just knew his head felt as if he'd suddenly walked into a wall. Luckily, he was close to home when it happened. He limped inside and described his symptoms to his wife, and they went to the ER.

Doctors performed a scan, revealing the rupture, and the next morning Warren had brain surgery.

Warren came out just fine, thank goodness. But what a close call. As if the experience weren't scary enough, it turns out that Warren hadn't been carrying any sort of identification at the time. He usually

(continued)

didn't when he ran. He easily could have collapsed miles from home, leaving EMTs to play detective just to figure out who the hell he was—much less who, if anyone, they should contact at home.

Today Warren wears an ID bracelet every time he puts on his running shoes. So do I. So should you. As far as peace of mind is concerned, it's probably the best investment a runner can make.

RULE 1.56

THE BEST JUKEBOX JUST MIGHT
BE IN YOUR HEAD

I NEVER RUN OUTDOORS WITH headphones. Ever.

Before you turn the page in disgust or gird yourself for a fight, let me assure you: This is not a rant against running with iPods. I learned long ago that no one on either side of that debate is likely to change his mind, no matter how compelling the argument.

Instead, this is simply my story. Take it for what it's worth.

Since long before there were iPods and Zunes and music-playing cell phones, I've been biking and running around with my own jukebox. In my head.

It's really pretty awesome.

My mental jukebox doesn't need batteries or a docking station. It never dies midrun or needs to sync up with my computer. I never forget it when I'm packing or heading out the door. And it's never made obsolete by a newer version.

It is completely wireless, weighs zero ounces, and is always there when I need it.

My mental jukebox also works beautifully in tandem with my body, sensing just what sort of tune I need to match the pace I'm running, then playing it. Because it's powered by my own weird brain (Subconsciousness Inside®), my mental jukebox also has a knack for surprising me with amusingly appropriate selections.

A few recent examples: During a tough speed workout on a winding trail, I glanced over my shoulder to see if a friend was gaining on me; in my head, I began to hear the chorus of Boston's

(continued)

"Don't Look Back." Midway through a group run along a twisty creekside path, I suddenly heard Creedence Clearwater Revival singing "Up Around the Bend"—as we ran, yes, around a bend. (Why my mental jukebox has been stuck in classic rock mode recently, I have no idea.)

And not for nothing, this particular music library allows total freedom of movement and interferes not one whit with any of my senses, keeping me aware of what's happening, 360 degrees.

Did I mention it's also free?

True, my mental jukebox isn't as sleek or sexy as the latest digital gizmo. But you know what? I wouldn't trade it for anything.

RULE 1.57

BEFORE A RACE OR LONG RUN, STRONG COFFEE IS YOUR BEST FRIEND

SCIENCE HAS SHOWN CAFFEINE to aid athletic performance. My own experience—and that of many runners before me—has shown coffee to provide another rather stimulating effect. And one that you might appreciate even more than the performance boost.

I won't get into the details here. Let's just say a cup or two of coffee about an hour before I run is part of my, um, regular routine.

Try it and see why.

RULE 1.58

A ROUTE IS A ROUTE WHEN IT BECOMES A ROUTE

I F THIS SOUNDS LIKE circular logic, that's because it is. It also happens to be the best answer to the question, "When does a running route, you know, become a *route*—as opposed to just the series of roads, streets, and paths you happen to be using for your run?"

Anyone who has run for any length of time knows what I'm talking about. A real running route, or "loop," is greater than the sum of its parts. A route has a history, a personality, a name. A route can be short and sweet or long and ugly, urban or rural, hilly or flat or rolling. A good route, over time, becomes another member of your running group. A good route wears a groove into your collective psyche.

So: How do you know when a route truly becomes a route? When two or more runners in your group can refer to it by name without confusion or further description.

When someone can suggest doing the Susan Seven, backward; or the Bait Shop Loop; or, simply, Fifth Street, and everyone else knows just what that means . . . congratulations. You have a route.

But not before.

5 WAYS TO NAME A ROUTE

1. Based on its shape, as seen from above—sort of the inverse of the way ancient cultures used to name constellations (e.g., the Phone Loop, which when seen from the sky looks like the outline of an old-fashioned telephone receiver)

2. Using the name of one or more of the streets or roads on the route (e.g., the Fifth Street Loop; Mill Road)

3. In honor of a landmark or town on or near the route (e.g., Bait Shop; Vera Cruz)

4. In honor of people—often the runner who discovered or popularized the route in question (e.g., the Susan Seven)

5. Based on something totally unimaginative, yet good to know (e.g., the Hill Loop)

RULE 1.59

KNOW THE DIFFERENCE BETWEEN
PAIN AND DISCOMFORT

A YOUNG ALAN WEBB, the prodigy who in 1999 broke Jim Ryun's high school mile record, once said of the tough training that lay ahead of him: "There will be a lot of suffering and discomfort. Let it hurt. Let it carry me to faster times."

Running is all about discomfort—seeking it, feeling it, managing it, overcoming it. And while pain inevitably and occasionally enters the picture (usually as you crest a long hill or kick to the finish line), it should never linger.

Only you can feel this distinction. Just try your best to recognize it and react accordingly: If what you're feeling is affecting your normal running form, or causing you genuine distress or fear for your well-being, then for goodness' sake, stop running and seek help.

Short of that? Hey, suck it up.

RULE 1.60

CHOOSE YOUR TATTOOS WISELY

T HIS IS ALWAYS GOOD advice, and not just for runners. That super-cool tribal tat you got at age 23 isn't going to look quite so super-cool when you're a sagging 85 and have to explain to yet another nurse that no, it is not a skin condition, it's a Polynesian symbol that means "free spirit." Tattoos for runners fall into two basic categories:

1. Running- or race-specific. We're talking here about those "26.2" tattoos or a little running guy on your ankle or—for a more select crowd—perhaps the Ironman logo. These are the equivalent of a bumper sticker that says I ♥ RUNNING. Except it's on your body, and you can't peel it off with a razor blade.

2. Generally cool and/or badass. These are tattoos that don't scream "running" or even necessarily whisper it. They're just cool. Typically they express, via words or symbols, the idea that the owner of the tat is disciplined or tough or otherwise up to the challenge. Think "fire-breathing dragon" or the words *up to the challenge.*

If you do decide to get a running tattoo, be sure you can back it up.

I have no tattoos, running or otherwise. If I did get one, it would likely be the Japanese characters meaning "wheeze."

The lesson here: Be wise. Think before you ink.

RULE 1.61

YOU'LL FIND THE ELUSIVE RUNNER'S HIGH WHEN YOU STOP LOOKING SO HARD FOR IT

THE RUNNER'S HIGH is like an orgasm.

Stop snickering! I'm serious.

The two phenomena are similar in the sense that they're physiological responses, intensely pleasurable, and—for some—maddeningly elusive. Some folks experience the runner's high regularly; for others, long or hard runs simply end in sweaty frustration. The act itself is fun, but, you know . . . anticlimactic.

No matter which climax is eluding you, the advice is basically the same: Relax. Stop focusing so much on the destination, and start focusing on the journey. Listen to your body. Breathe. Enjoy yourself. You'll get there.

Now, about those multiple runner's highs . . .

RULE 1.62

HAVING A MILLION THINGS TO DO IS AN EXCUSE *FOR* RUNNING, NOT AN ARGUMENT AGAINST IT

THERE ARE A HUNDRED excuses not to run. Being busy just isn't one of them. Why? Because taking even 20 or 30 minutes for a run will help you organize your thoughts, clear your head, wake up, and return to your tasks with a clarity and energy you can't get from coffee or even a nap.

So if you're feeling overwhelmed or overbooked, put the to-do list down and lace up your running shoes. You'll be glad you did.

RULE 1.63

BE COOL WHEN YOU
MEET AN ELITE

A MONG MOST SPORTS, road racing is uniquely egalitarian. You get to run the same race as the most elite of the elites, on the same course and the same clock. You cross the same finish line, albeit minutes or hours later.

This has been noted, and celebrated, many times by many authors.

What hasn't been explored, in any satisfactory way, is how you should behave when you encounter one of these elite runners. Here's what is ok, and what is not.

ACCEPTABLE BEHAVIOR	UNACCEPTABLE BEHAVIOR
• Smiling and/or waving at the athlete	• Offering the athlete training advice
• Telling him or her that you are a "big fan"	• Asking the athlete how much he or she earns
• Congratulating him or her on a recent performance	• Becoming so anxious that you vomit on the athlete
• Wishing him or her luck on an upcoming performance	• Asking him or her to sign any part of your body typically covered by beachwear
• Asking for a photo and/or an autograph, if the time and place are appropriate (i.e., not while the athlete is dining or worshipping or sleeping or bathing or racing)	• Kissing
	• Requesting a lock of hair
	• Trying to bum 20 bucks

RULE 1.64

CONCRETE ISN'T REALLY
HARDER THAN ASPHALT

THIS IS ONE OF THOSE old canards you'll hear from time to time, usually from defensive runners answering critics who say they should be running on the sidewalk.

"I'm a road runner," they'll sniff. "I run on roads."

And then, for good measure: "Besides, running on concrete is less forgiving than running on the road."

Bull hooey.

Scientists with precise instruments may be able to measure differences in the shock absorption of concrete versus asphalt. But unless you're running exclusively on concrete, or for miles at a time on the stuff, your joints will never know the difference.

If you want an excuse not to run on sidewalks, try the "debris/pedestrians/cracks" angle.

And either way, watch out for those scientists.

RULE 1.65

WARN BEFORE PASSING

A S A RUNNER, YOU will pass other runners. This will happen no matter how slow you happen to be because there will always be someone slower than you are (page 52). As a courtesy, you should first alert them to your presence.

The proper distance from which to issue this warning is 12 to 25 feet, depending on your speed relative to the runner being passed. The greater your speed, the earlier you'll want to issue the warning. The idea is for the passer to give the passee's brain enough time to process the warning before the actual passing occurs.

The warning can take any number of forms: a cough, a shuffling of your feet, a verbal heads-up such as "Heads up!" Sometimes something as simple and subtle as a loud sniff can work. Other times—for instance, in a relatively loud, crowded park—you might want to ramp things up with a polite "Excuse me!" or "Passing on your left!" It's a judgment call.

Note: Handheld air horns are not an acceptable form of warning. Even if they are hilarious.

RULE 1.66

DOGS ARE HARMLESS,
EXCEPT WHEN THEY AREN'T

M OST DOGS, WHEN THEY SEE a passing runner, will bark. This is the natural order of things. Just continue along your way—and don't make eye contact with the dog, which he may consider threatening. The dog will yap until you're out of sight or until something else captures his attention, such as a blade of grass. And that will be that.

Occasionally, however, you may encounter a dog who is not content simply to bark at you, but who wants to put parts of your body between his teeth. Dogs like this are known, in veterinary science, as bad dogs.

Avoid such dogs whenever possible.

If an aggressive dog does threaten you, yell "No!" in a deep voice and try to put something between you and the dog, such as a bicycle or a small child.

Just kidding about the small child. They can bite, too. And they don't recognize the word *no*.

HARMLESS

VICIOUS

RULE 1.67

NEVER UNDERESTIMATE
THE VALUE OF A TRITE SLOGAN

DON'T ASK ME WHY, but the sappiest, most maudlin dime-store platitude—when used in the context of running—can be genuinely inspirational. It's a kind of alchemy.

I'm talking here about such phrases as, "Pain is temporary. Quitting lasts forever." Or "Adversity causes some men to break, and others to break records." Heard anywhere else, such corny aphorisms might inspire eye rolling. But, for whatever reason, seen or heard in or around a race, they work.

I distinctly recall running a half-marathon near my home in eastern Pennsylvania. It was somewhere between miles 10 and 11, and I was starting to hurt, running nearly alone at that point and fighting the urge to ease up and just coast to the finish. Who would know? And what difference would it make?

That's when I looked up and noticed the back of another runner's shirt. On it was a quote from Steve Prefontaine (page 12): "To give anything less than your best is to sacrifice the gift."

I nearly cried. Seriously.

Oh, and if you want a slogan that's not trite, try this one, attributed to Benjamin Franklin:

"Things that hurt, instruct."

I'm pretty sure Ben wasn't a runner. But that quote makes you wonder.

RULE 1.68

IMAGINE THE WORST

I HATE TO SOUND PESSIMISTIC. Really, I do. But thinking in terms of worst-case scenarios can make you a happier, healthier runner. This rule holds true across a variety of everyday situations, in decisions large and small. For instance:

"I bet I can make it through this intersection before that RV does."
BEST CASE: You sprint across the road and save a few moments.
WORST CASE: You sprint into the road and die.
FINAL CALL: Wait.

"I probably won't need a hat in the race this weekend."
BEST CASE: You leave the hat at home, do not in fact need it, and your suitcase is 2 ounces lighter.
WORST CASE: You leave the hat at home, wake up on race day to record-low temperatures, drop out at mile 9 with hypothermia, and find yourself being "warmed up" by a race volunteer who smells like garlic.
FINAL CALL: Pack the hat.

"You know, I usually eat oatmeal before a long run, but those leftover chalupas are looking pretty good."
BEST CASE: You consume the leftover chalupas and complete your long run as planned.
WORST CASE: You consume the leftover chalupas, begin your long run as planned, and end it 2 miles later, doubled over and feeling as if Satan himself is traveling through your lower intestine with a pitchfork made of fire and dipped in taco sauce.
FINAL CALL: Boil some water because you're taking the whole grain train to Quaker-town.

The list goes on and on. But you get the idea: Prepare for the worst; hope for the best. And stick to oatmeal.

THE 7 DEADLY SINS: RUNNING EDITION

1. LUST
MANIFESTATION: Drooling over the new Kayanos when the ones you have now are perfectly fine

2. GLUTTONY
MANIFESTATION: Grabbing more banana halves and bagels from the postrace food table than you could ever hope to eat

3. GREED
MANIFESTATION: Selling your Boston finisher's medal on eBay; trying to unload your NYC Marathon entry to some desperate soul for double what you paid for it

4. SLOTH
MANIFESTATION: I think we all know what this one looks like.

5. WRATH
MANIFESTATION: Losing your cool when the guy at the running store says the new Kayanos are sold out in your size, and they aren't expecting another shipment for 6 weeks

6. ENVY
MANIFESTATION: Coveting thy neighbor's wife's half-marathon PR

7. PRIDE
MANIFESTATION: Checking your appearance in every storefront window that you run past

RACING, TRACK WORKOUTS, AND OTHER FORMS OF DISCOMFORT

IN WHICH WE examine bibs, bandits, postrace bagels, corner-cutting, hideous race photos, the Stallone Constant, and the meaning of that mysterious NO TRESPASSING sign at the local track.

RULE 2.1A

DON'T COMPLAIN
ABOUT THE RACE ENTRY FEE

HEY, NO ONE IS holding a gun to your head. (And if they are, you've got bigger problems.) Don't like the fee? Find a smaller (read: cheaper) race. But whatever you do . . .

RULE 2.1B

PAY YOUR WAY

BANDIT A RACE, and you're stealing, pure and simple.
If you're preparing a spirited defense—a laundry list of all the rationalizations you've dreamed up to justify running a race without paying for it—save your breath. I've heard 'em all. And they're all nonsense.

Staging a race costs real money. If you can't afford to pay your share, there are plenty of other roads for you to use on race day.

Running is free. Racing is not.

RULE 2.2

TO TRULY KNOW SOMEONE,
RUN A RELAY RACE WITH HIM

E VENTS LIKE OREGON'S Hood to Coast Relay—a 197-mile race from Mount Hood to the Pacific Ocean, usually done in teams of 12—are unbelievably fun. And challenging. And a great way to find out what someone's really made of.

Nothing strips away the artifice and reveals your friends' true nature quite like spending 24 or so sleep-deprived hours with them in a van full of sweat, gear bags, pretzel crumbs, and door handles made sticky by Cherry Coke.

Somewhere out there on God-knows-what-rural-route, in that van at 3:30 a.m., cramped and cranky and struggling to get some sort of rest in between legs, you get a rare glimpse of man at his best. And worst. And smelliest.

RULE 2.3

MAKE A PACKING LIST

Y<small>ES, IT'S NERDY.</small> But making a race weekend packing checklist can save your neck. And nothing—*nothing*—is too obvious for the checklist, up to and including your running shoes.

Depending on how far you're traveling for your event—and the season—here are a few items you might consider including.

RUNNING STUFF

- ☐ Running shoes (plus extra pair)
- ☐ Light running jacket and/or vest
- ☐ Race-day apparel
- ☐ Extra running shirts and shorts
- ☐ Running socks
- ☐ Fleece pullover or insulated jacket

- ☐ Running pants or tights
- ☐ Running watch (plus extra, if you have one)
- ☐ ID bracelet
- ☐ Sunglasses
- ☐ Knit cap
- ☐ Running cap with visor
- ☐ Thin gloves

NUTRITION

- ☐ Race-day gels, beans, or bars (if you plan to carry some)
- ☐ Sports drink or drink mix of choice

- ☐ Healthy snacks for trip (fruit, fig bars, pretzels, etc.)
- ☐ Any special prerace foods you might not be able to find locally

---

ELECTRONICS

- ☐ Cell phone
- ☐ Cell phone charger
- ☐ MP3 player
- ☐ MP3 player dock and/or charger
- ☐ Travel alarm clock

MISCELLANEOUS

- ☐ Reading material (to keep your mind off the race, if need be)
- ☐ Large garbage bag (in case of rain)
- ☐ Directions to race expo
- ☐ Registration/ confirmation card
- ☐ Band-Aids
- ☐ Extra safety pins
- ☐ Petroleum jelly or body lube
- ☐ Antacid tablets

ON A RELATED NOTE: Don't forget the even more obvious stuff. I work with a woman—an experienced marathoner, by the way—who once trained meticulously for a marathon in a faraway state, tapered well, packed carefully, made the trip, and realized that *she had forgotten to register for the race.*

Whoops.

RULE 2.4

APPROACH THE EXPO
WITH CAUTION

R ACE EXPOS ARE MYSTICAL places where the usual laws of retail and consumption do not apply.

Don't need another singlet? Another pair of shorts or tights or shoes? Another bagful of energy gels or a new pair of shades?

Who cares! You're at the expo! You've trained hard to get here and denied yourself for months and months. Now it's your weekend, dammit, and you owe it to yourself to indulge a little in the form of purchasing that commemorative race plaque, those hats, and this what-the-heck-is-this-thing, anyway? You know what? Who cares what it is? You'll take it!

If you have the disposable income to handle this sort of indiscriminate splurging on stuff you frankly don't need, then have at it. Enjoy.

RULE 2.5

THE WHOLE PASTA THING
IS WAY OVERBLOWN

DISTANCE RUNNING AND PASTA are so closely associated, it makes you wonder if the two industries aren't in cahoots. (It's probably a coincidence that the last journalist to explore this theory was found dead soon after he starting asking questions, buried under 3 tons of elbow macaroni in a Long Island warehouse.)

I should stress that eating pasta the night before a long race is not a bad idea. It's great, if that's what you're hungry for. Or what you're used to. I often enjoy a plate of penne as a prerace dinner.

But there's nothing magical about the stuff. It's just flour and water, folks.

So have whatever you like the night before a race, assuming it's reasonably healthy and reasonably "safe." (Steak tartare is probably not the smartest choice, nor is the habañero bean burrito platter at that new hole-in-the-wall Mexican joint.) And for Pete's sake, don't eat anything you've never tried before.

Don't overthink. Let your gut guide you. You'll be fine.

RULE 2.6

TAKE PRERACE DREAMS
IN STRIDE

YOU'RE RUNNING—OR TRYING TO—AND it feels like you're chest-deep in molasses. You want to run normally but you can't, no matter how hard you try. In fact, the harder you try, the harder it becomes. Your muscles just don't respond. Your joints feel petrified, and your limbs only work against you.

Every inch of every step is a struggle, and it's exhausting.

Sound familiar? It sure does to me. I often have a dream like this in the weeks leading up to a race—or even when no race is planned at all. Most runners seem to. The culprit may be plain-vanilla anxiety, or something called REM paralysis, wherein your muscles actually do feel immobilized temporarily.

Either way, it's nothing to worry about. In fact, it's normal. Ditto for dreams where you're a mile from the starting line when you hear the gun go off, or where you're frantically searching for your racing shoes moments before the start, and so on.

Do your best to shrug off such dreams, chalking them up to normal mental preparation for a big event.

Oh, and that dream where your mother is chasing you through an amusement park on horseback? Sorry. You're on your own with that one.

RULE 2.7

WRITE ON YOUR BIB

YOU KNOW THAT FORM on the flip side of your bib number? The one that includes blank lines for info like your name, address, and emergency contact? Yeah. Fill it out.

I know, I know. It's silly. And a pain in the neck. (Where's a ballpoint pen when you need one?) And chances are excellent that it will never make a difference.

But maybe one of these times, it will.

Take a minute, find a ballpoint or a Sharpie, and fill it out. You'll feel better. Your loved ones will feel better. The race's medical director will feel better. And the ballpoint pen industry will definitely feel better.

It's a win-win-win-win!

RULE 2.8

BIB NUMBERS GO ON THE FRONT

NOT ON YOUR BUTT or on the back of your shirt. On the front. Otherwise, you'll look like a bandit (page 158) to every race official who sees you coming.

Worse, how will the race photographers identify you? How?!

RULE 2.9

LEARN TO LOVE
"RACE MORNING BUZZ"

THAT'S THE QUIETLY ELECTRIC aura of anticipation that surrounds you the morning of a race, beginning the instant you wake up and lasting till the gun fires at the starting line. It's a background hum of energy, a tickle almost. Combined with the stillness of early morning prerace ritual, it's one of the best feelings you'll ever encounter.

It really is impossible to do "race morning buzz" justice with mere words. Let's just say that you'll know it when you feel it. You'll wish there was a way to bottle it, so you could have a little bit every day. But there's not. Which is probably for the best.

Instead, savor it while you can. Drink it in.

Then take a deep breath—and race.

RULE 2.10

DOUBLE KNOT BEFORE THE GUN

O F ALL THE FOREHEAD-SLAPPINGLY preventable snafus encountered during a race, the untied shoelace has to be at the top of the list. This one has bedeviled elites as well as amateurs, and there is absolutely no excuse for it.

Do yourself a favor and take a few extra seconds to double knot your laces after your warmup.

RULE 2.11

REMOVE YOUR HAT WHEN THEY PLAY THE NATIONAL ANTHEM

MANNERS AND COMMON COURTESY apply, even during a race, and even when your hat is made of technical sweat-wicking fabrics. Show some respect.

RULE 2.12

WRITE OFF THE FIRST MILE

THE FIRST MILE OR so of any large race is pandemonium, as folks ride a surge of pent-up adrenaline and try to run half a step in front of everyone else.

You'll see a lot of frantic people jockeying for position during those first few minutes. Ignore them. Be cool. Run your own race. The people sprinting, weaving, and darting around you are wasting tons of energy, and you'll likely pass them later. Probably sooner than you think.

RULE 2.13A

FIGHT THE URGE TO DROP OUT

I F YOU'RE DOING IT RIGHT, at some point you will want to drop out of just about every race you run. This is normal. Recognize this fact and expect it. During your training, anticipate how you'll respond when this happens, when your body rebels and your mind urges you to stop.

RULE 2.13B

BUT IF YOU DO DROP OUT, MAKE PEACE WITH YOUR DECISION

D ON'T DWELL ON A DNF, a "Did Not Finish." Chalk it up to experience, and vow to train and race smarter next time. What's done is done, and you've lived to race another day. So be it.

RULE 2.14

ACKNOWLEDGE BANDS
ALONG THE COURSE

A S A GROUP, MUSICIANS do not like to wake up early. But these particular musicians did just that, loading their vans in the predawn darkness, driving to whatever godforsaken mile marker they've been assigned to, setting up their stuff, and *rocking out.*

Or, you know, *jazzing out.* Or *tribal drumming out, bluesing out, calypsoing out.* The point is, they are out there for you, playing their hearts out so that you may be motivated. And you really should acknowledge them to the best of your ability.

Just how you acknowledge them depends on how fast you're going and/or how much you're suffering. Use this chart for guidance.

SPEED/SUFFERING

LOW		HIGH
stop, listen, applaud	thumbs-up or peace sign	nod head

RULE 2.15

YOU WILL HEAR THE THEME
FROM *ROCKY*

FOR ROAD RACERS, HEARING THE THEME from *Rocky* isn't a question of "if," but "when."

During any given race, the chance that you will hear the theme from *Rocky* blaring at the start/finish line, or from a spectator's stereo along the course is 75 percent. If the race is in Philadelphia, that probability soars to 98 percent.

Little-known fact: Regardless of location, age, gender, ethnicity, or income, precisely 67 percent of runners will react to hearing the *Rocky* theme during a race by raising both arms and pumping their fists.

This is the real-world manifestation of what mathematicians call the Stallone Constant.

Strange but true!*

*This is not true.

RULE 2.16

KEEP IT CLEAN

RACES ARE FAMILY-FRIENDLY AFFAIRS . . . or should be. This doesn't mean that every second of every race needs to be squeaky clean. But please, for the sake of community standards and for the occasional tender ear among you, keep the four-letter words to a minimum.

Think of a race like an outing to the movies, except instead of watching a film and munching popcorn, a bunch of strangers have gathered to breathe hard and spill Gatorade down their chests.

Here's a useful rule of thumb: If you wouldn't blurt it out during a *Harry Potter* matinee, try not to do so at a race.

RULE 2.17

HAVE A MANTRA

"NOTHING WORTHWHILE IS EASY." . . . "Do it for [insert name here]." . . . "One more mile." . . . "Loose and strong."

No matter what phrase you choose, it's always nice to have a mantra to fall back on when the going gets tough. Repeating the same few words to yourself can serve as a focal point—or as a distraction, depending on how you look at it. This works even better if you use this same mantra during hard workouts and long runs during training. (Some folks—myself included—will tell you that finding and using a good mantra should, in fact, be part of your training.)

A single word can be just as effective, by the way. *Smooth,* for example. Or *light.* Or *beer.* (But not *lite beer.* That's just weak.)

RULE 2.18

LINE UP WHERE YOU BELONG

WANT TO WITNESS a fascinating sociological experiment? Head for the starting line of any race large enough to have signs indicating "pace per mile." Notice the large signs reading "5:00" (meaning 5 minutes per mile), "6:00" (6 minutes per mile), "7:00," and so on.

Then have a look at the folks clustering around these signs. You never knew there were so many fast runners, did you?

Well, here's a little secret: There aren't.

Many of the runners lined up at such signs really are that fast and really do expect to run at or around that pace during the race. The rest are either delusional or just plain rude.

You know how fast you can expect to run on any given day, give or take. Be honest with yourself, and fair to your fellow runners. Line up where you belong.

RULE 2.19

COVER YOUR CHEST

Guys: RUNNING WITHOUT A SHIRT is okay; racing without a shirt is tacky.

There's no satisfactory way we can explain why this is. It's just one of those things.

A routine run on a hot summer day is a fine time to go shirtless, assuming you have the upper body to pull it off and/or the confidence to do so.

Racing, though, that's different.

Maybe it's the sacred nature of a race (Would you go shirtless in church?), or maybe it's the mere fact that so many eyes are on you all at once, or maybe it's a bit of both.

Whatever the reason, racing simply calls for covering your nipples. It's the right thing to do.

Besides: Pinning your bib number to your chest is much more pleasant if you're wearing a top.

RULE 2.20

"LOOKIN' GOOD"...
AND 10 OTHER LIES RUNNERS
TELL EACH OTHER

LYING IS NOT SOMETHING we endorse under normal circumstances. But racing is not normal. This is why it's perfectly acceptable—admirable, even—to tell a fellow runner that he is looking good at mile 19 of a marathon when, in fact, he looks like an insomniac zombie who's trying to sneeze but can't, and is confused because someone has apparently switched his normal running shoes with exact replicas made of concrete.

In cases like this, by all means, lie.

The "go-to" lie in these situations is that old standby, "Lookin' good!" Variations include: "You look *great!*" ... "Lookin' smooth!" and the hybrid "You're lookin' *great!*" Then there's the cruelest lie of all: "You're almost there!" (In a marathon, you may hear this one as early as mile 7.)

These lies are all well and good. In fact, a race wouldn't be a race without them. But if you'd like to try something more original, try one of these.

- "You look so smooth, I suspect someone has sprayed your joints with PAM™ cooking spray!" (Yes, you must include the ™ when you say this.)

- "I am tempted to alert a race official because I could swear that you just walked onto the course, rather than starting with those around you. That is how fresh you look!"

- "If I weren't so awed by the apparent ease with which you're navigating this course, I might be angry with you for nearly knocking me unconscious . . . with your very awesomeness!"

- "From just the right angle, I'm fairly certain I can detect an actual, visible aura of strength and fluidity surrounding you like a halo! Continue running so that others may bask in it!"

- "Go in grace, you lithesome creature of God! Your very presence elevates this road race to levels sublime!"

And if you just cannot bring yourself to lie, there are always these truth-neutral chestnuts: "Keep it up!" and "*Wo-o-o-o-o-o!*"

Truth, fiction, or neutral, the key is to say *something*. Even a zombie appreciates a note of encouragement.

RULE 2.21

"HOLDING IT" IS ALWAYS
A CRAP SHOOT

IT'S INEVITABLE: SOMEDAY, SOMEWHERE, you will be racing and feel a rumble in your gut. You will wait for the rumble to go away. It won't. Instead, it will gradually worsen—well, "gradually" if you're lucky—into a familiar, uncomfortable, and very unwelcome pressure deep inside you.

Soon enough, you will spot a porta potty along the course—again, if you're lucky. And you will face a sudden, stark choice: *Do I stop for a few minutes, possibly blowing my race and/or missing a time goal, to take care of this? Or do I press on, and hope for the best?*

This is a question only you can answer. Only you will know the severity of the discomfort, the urgency of relieving it, and the importance to you of that particular race.

Personally? I typically err on the side of getting relief while the getting is good. Haven't regretted it yet. And to be honest, neither has anyone around me.

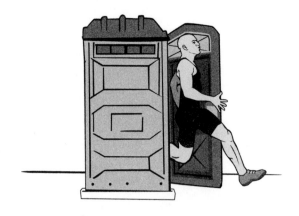

RULE 2.22

AVOID CRASHING

AND WE DON'T MEAN the "hitting the wall/running out of energy" kind.

Most people don't associate footraces with crashes, the way they might with bike racing or stock-car racing or downhill skiing. But even runners can go down during a race, alone or in a pileup.

Usually this occurs during crowded starts, when adrenaline and flailing limbs can combine with unpleasant results; in a race's latter stages (particularly the final stretch), as exhausted runners lose fine motor skills, and small cracks and bumps in the road seem to reach out and grab you; and whenever several runners stream around a sharp corner.

All it takes is one clipped heel and *wham*. You collide with another runner or with the road. Or both. You won't cartwheel down the street and burst into flames, the way a NASCAR driver might. (Wouldn't that do wonders for marathon spectating, though?) But it sure can result in some nasty road rash.

So: Keep your wits about you, and keep some distance between yourself and the runner in front of you.

RULE 2.23

DON'T RATTLE, JINGLE, OR JANGLE

A S A COURTESY TO the runners around you—and as a measure of self-preservation—make an effort to secure the stuff in your pockets or waist pack. This means everything from keys and loose change to Sport Beans and pills. This is especially true during a long run or race; nobody wants to run next to someone who sounds like a giant box of Tic Tacs.

If you do all of this and still hear a rattling or jangling sound when you run, see a physician.

Exception: I once ran with a heart attack survivor who produced a chik-chik-chik sound with each step. The noise, he explained, was a tiny bottle of nitroglycerin tablets in his pocket. In the event of another heart attack, his instructions were to swallow the nitro. Folks like this have earned the right to rattle when they run.

RULE 2.24

STAY ON COURSE

RACE COURSES ARE MEASURED on the tangents—that is, assuming the shortest line around corners and bends. This means that the best, fastest possible way for you to take a turn involves "running" or "cutting" the tangent: You start near the center of the road, then aim to hit the corner right *on* the corner before swinging back out. (If you ever want to see this done beautifully and at greater speeds, watch a multilap, or "criterium," bike race.)

What this does not mean is that you should hop the curb, run on the sidewalk, or otherwise leave the course itself to shave a few seconds off your time, or avoid the rest of us suckers who are actually bothering to follow the rules.

Yes, that is cheating. And yes, it does matter.

RULE 2.25

NEVER MISS A CHANCE
TO THANK A VOLUNTEER

EVEN IF YOU'RE RUNNING the race of your life and trying to make every movement count, you can still manage a bit of eye contact and a nod as you grab a cup of water from an outstretched hand. Even if it feels like your quads are quite literally on fire, you can manage to sputter a short "thanks" to the course marshal standing in the intersection.

It will make the volunteer feel good. It will make you feel good. Try it.

RULE 2.26

PEE IF YOU MUST

IF THIS WERE A rule book for humans at large, one of the first rules would have to be: *When You've Gotta Go, You've Gotta Go.* This goes double for tightly wound, highly hydrated, slightly nervous humans who are standing around (i.e., runners waiting for a race to start). If you simply can't hold it any longer, do your best to locate a porta potty. Failing that, find a stand of trees or bushes as far from the action as reasonably possible. Failing *that*—if, for instance, you're stuck in the middle of a packed corral at the start of a large marathon and you're about to burst—well, pop a squat or take a knee, and do what you've gotta do. Be as discreet as possible, apologize to those around you, then stand up, and return your focus to the race.

And before your next race, hydrate just a little bit less.

RULE 2.27

RUN THE MILE YOU'RE IN

ESPECIALLY FOR LONGER RACES (but even for short ones, like 5-Ks), it can be tempting to dwell on the total distance or on how far you are from the finish line. Try not to. Instead, focus on the mile you're running at that particular moment.

Be mindful of the full distance, of course; mentally and physically, you should be aware of how far you've got to go. Primarily, though, keep your head in the here and now.

That's a nice metaphor for life, too, by the way. In case you were looking for one.

RULE 2.28

RELAX

THIS JUST MIGHT BE the single most useful rule about racing. And it works on more than one level.

- Relax in the buildup to your race: Added tension and anxiety can only hurt you.

- Relax the night before your race: At this late stage, you've either trained enough to meet your goals or you haven't; things are in fate's hands now. And there's a certain relief in that. Take advantage of this relief to get some much-deserved rest.

- Relax in the hours just before your race: Apart from a brief warmup walk/jog, spend this time thinking pleasant thoughts—or not thinking at all. Focus on running a smooth, fast race. Visualize yourself smiling on the course. Imagine the finish line, and yourself gliding across it. Then go do it.

- Relax during the race: Clenched fists and hunched shoulders will only sap energy that should be devoted to moving you forward.

Oh, and don't forget to relax postrace, with the recovery beverage of your choice. My personal favorite is Blue Point Toasted Lager.

RULE 2.29

PRETEND YOU'RE BRITISH

RUNNERS AT THE START of a race can be testy for the same reasons they can have overactive bladders: They're pumped up yet caged up; they're a bit anxious; and the adrenaline is flowing. Then the gun goes off. Suddenly, folks who were bumping elbows just a few seconds ago are moving forward in a knot, trying to pass each other.

No wonder tempers can flare, particularly in the first mile or so. One smart way to react, should you ever be on the receiving end of a flare-up: Go all British on 'em. Not in a cockney-accent, tea-drinking kind of way . . . but in that unfailingly polite and unassuming kind of way.

Nothing disarms people or diffuses tension faster than a smile and a "sorry" or "my fault." Holding a hand up, palm facing out, doesn't hurt, either. It's a universal symbol for "I come in peace and am sorry for kicking the back of your shoe."

RULE 2.30

RACES ARE ALL ABOUT
ENERGY MANAGEMENT

I DON'T KNOW WHO WAS the first to say this, but truer words were never spoken.

The only thing worse than running out of energy a mile from the finish line is finishing the race with energy left over.

RULE 2.31

KEEP MOVING FORWARD

YOU'RE IN YOUR CAR, zipping down the highway in rush-hour traffic, when a pack of gum or a bottle cap gets away from you and flies out the window. Do you slam on the brakes? Do a U-turn and thread your way through the oncoming cars to retrieve your lost goods?

Not if you're sober, you don't.

So why on earth would you do it in a race? The consequences when you're running aren't deadly, of course, but they could be injurious. And even if no collision occurs, it's highly annoying to see someone freeze in the middle of a pack to pick up a gel packet or a glove.

Don't be that person. Let it go. Or—if your lost item is valuable enough—step off the course as soon as you safely can, then walk back along the side of the road to pick it up.

If you can, apologize . . . with a British accent.

RULE 2.32

DO WHATEVER IT TAKES
TO FINISH AHEAD
OF A COSTUMED RUNNER

B ECAUSE BEING OUTKICKED BY Elmo is too much to bear.

RULE 2.33

BE CORDIAL WITH YOUR RIVALS

D ID YOU SHADOW ANOTHER runner in the final stretch of your race, or vice versa? Perhaps pushing each other to go a bit faster or out-and-out fighting to be first to the line? Good for you. (Both of you!) This competitive give-and-take is one of the best parts of racing.

Once you've crossed the line, a gracious gesture is always appropriate. Offer a kind word, an open hand, or a pat on the back to anyone who was with you in those closing minutes of your race. Whether you egged each other on verbally, or wordlessly coaxed a bit more kick out of each other, you've just shared a bit of sportsmanship that deserves to be noted.

Hugs and kisses? Maybe not—unless your rival is also a spouse or significant other. Or European. Or both.

RULE 2.34

PLEASE, NO PUSHUPS
ON THE FINISH LINE

FIRST OF ALL: IF YOU HAVE ENERGY enough to pump out pushups the moment you finish a race, you haven't raced hard enough. You shouldn't be showboating; you should be kicking yourself and vowing to do better next time.

Second, and from a more pragmatic point of view: Doing pushups at the finish line—or, worse, *on* the finish line—puts you at real risk for being stepped on . . . "accidentally."

And there's not a jury or a race director in the land who would side with you in a situation like that.

RULE 2.35

SCOOT THROUGH THE CHUTE

DON'T CLOG UP THE finish line chute if you can help it. Keep moving as best you can. If you're wearing a timing chip that must be snipped off, follow the same rule that you do with aid station tables: Pass the first one and the second and third ones. Everyone else will clump around them. Keep moving, and approach a volunteer snipper a bit farther down the line.

RULE 2.36

POSTRACE BAGELS MUST BE DRY
AND TASTE LIKE ASPIRIN

N O ONE KNOWS WHY this is a rule. But, judging from every single postrace bagel I have ever tried, it is.

RULE 2.37

YOUR MEDAL IS WEARABLE
FOR A REASON

WILL YOU LOOK A little cheesy walking (or limping) around town postrace with a—let's face it—chintzy medal hanging from your neck? Yes. Should that dissuade you from doing so? No way. You've earned the right to indulge in a little cheesiness.

So go for it. Loop that thing around your neck. Wear it after the race, wear it out to dinner that night—heck, wear it to work the next morning. Anyone who wants to judge you can do so just as soon as they earn their own medals.

RULE 2.38

RACE PHOTOS NEVER
LOOK GOOD

A ND I MEAN NEVER.
  Brad Pitt could show up at the start of a marathon completely rested, tanned, toned, massaged, hydrated, and professionally
styled, and by the time the race photographer snapped him at mile
13, he would . . . well, he would probably look pretty good. He is
Brad Pitt, after all.

But the photos of Brad Pitt, when he finally saw them, would
look horrible. In the photos, Brad would look like a badly dehy-
drated Quasimodo having a seizure. This is the magic of race pho-
tography. If the folks who sold race photos were smart, they'd charge
people *not* to send prints of their pics.

That said, should you order some of these race photos anyway?
Absolutely. And the bigger, the better.

RULE 2.39

YOU MUST RUN AT LEAST ONE RACE
IN YOUR LIFETIME
THAT FINISHES ON A TRACK

SERIOUSLY. It's really something.

RULE 2.40

RESPECT THE RULES
OF THE TRACK

Here's a rule of thumb: If you have to hop a fence or squeeze through a gate in order to run on a track, it is not okay for you to run on that track.

What's that? You say the track belongs to a public school, and your tax dollars pay for it? Sorry. Tax dollars pay for lots of stuff that is off-limits to the average civilian. The Oval Office, for instance.

No one else is there, and it's a crime for such a fine track to go unused? Tell that to the folks who locked the place up and posted the No Trespassing signs.

If you want to work out on a track, contact a local school and seek permission; they just might grant it. Or go through your friendly neighborhood running club. They'll likely have a list of publicly available tracks.

RULE 2.41

RUN IN THE INNER LANES;
RECOVER IN THE OUTER

J UST LIKE WITH HIGHWAY driving, rules exist on the track to make behavior predictable and, therefore, conditions safer for everyone. The most fundamental, universal rule: Fast runners stick to the inside lanes. Slower runners or walkers occupy the outer ones.

RULE 2.42

NO BARKING

YES, WE KNOW, THE adrenaline is flowing and the lactic acid is like battery acid in your veins, but please, be courteous. No need to snarl "On your right!" or "On your left!" as you brush past slower runners or even (gasp!) walkers on the track.

Shouting "Track!" is worse, as 99 laypersons out of 100 will have absolutely no idea what you're saying, and will probably just turn around, bemused, directly into your path.

If the track is really that crowded, and you really fear a collision, do what you would do off the track to alert others to your presence: Clear your throat or cough as you approach.

And give those slower, unfortunate folks wide enough berth as you pass. There's room for both of you. And who knows? One day, you might just be the one "in the way."

RULE 2.43

NO SPITTING ON THE TRACK

HOLD IT IN, PLEASE. If you can't, at least spit into the infield. Or onto someone who's barking, "On your left!"

(Just kidding.)

(Not really.)

RULE 2.44

BECOMING A HUMAN
METRONOME IS FUN

RUNNING ON A TRACK can be deathly monotonous. But there's a payoff, too, if you're patient enough to discover it. That payoff? Becoming a human metronome.

By that I mean learning to sense your own pace, to the point where you can run scary-precise splits for quarter-mile after quarter-mile, without even looking at your watch.

It doesn't come easy. And, depending on how often you're able to run on a track and how disciplined you are, it might not come at all. But for those who are willing to put in the time and work at it, developing this talent can be pretty satisfying.

It works, of course, by paying close attention to your watch—at first—on every 200- or 400-meter repeat. Gradually you'll notice that your times are grouping closer and closer to a single mean. Soon you'll discover that you're nailing this time, or something very close to it, without using your watch at all.

This means that you're getting a better feel for pace and meting out effort and all that stuff. Which is good.

Me, I just think it's cool.

RULE 2.45

WHEN YOU'VE FINISHED, WIPE THE TRACK DOWN FOR THE NEXT RUNNER

O KAY, JUST KIDDING.

SHOES, APPAREL, AND GEAR

I N THIS CHAPTER: Billed caps, short shorts vs. long shorts, race-shirt faux pas, new-shoe smell, wardrobe diversity, and more. Plus: Cotton—hot or not?

RULE 3.1

CALL THEM RUNNING SHOES

THEY AREN'T SNEAKERS or tennis shoes or kicks or trainers (sorry, Brits). They are running shoes. So call them that.

RULE 3.2

BEFORE YOU REMOVE NEW RUNNING SHOES FROM THE BOX, YOU MUST SMELL THEM

OPEN THE BOX. PEEL BACK the tissue paper. Behold those pristine shoes. Then lift the box to your face and breathe deeply. *Mm-m-m.* Smells like . . . potential.

And possibly formaldehyde or something. But mostly potential.

RULE 3.3

DON'T DRESS LIKE A NINJA

YOU KNOW WHAT I'M talking about: the dressed-head-to-toe-in-black thing. Black tights. Black shirt or jacket. Black gloves. Black hat.

It seems that many runners are darting around dressed like this, even at night or when visibility is very low. I'm noticing more and more of them each year.

And those are only the ones I can see.

I first noticed this trend while living in Manhattan. But then, a black outfit seems to be the de facto uniform of New Yorkers, so it seemed only logical that NYC runners would dress that way, even at night. And even if it renders them near invisible to insane bike messengers and cell-phone-chatting cab drivers.

But now it seems the trend is spreading. Why?

Is it because black is slimming? Because it hides stains? Because it makes "matching" a no-brainer? (And should I say something to the invisible man who runs by me at 9 p.m.? Like "Friend, are you aware that what you're wearing is essentially nighttime camouflage? And that many cars weigh 2 tons?")

Maybe the simplest explanation here really is the correct one: These guys aren't runners. They really *are* ninjas, out doing roadwork.

If that's the case, I think I'll just let them be.

RULE 3.4

BE AT PEACE
WITH YOUR SHORTS

RUNNING SHORTS ARE an outward barometer of modesty. That's a polite way of saying, "When it comes to shorts, go as long—or as short—as you like. We won't judge."

The length of running shorts isn't really a fashion thing, the way hemlines or necktie widths are. There have always been short shorts and long baggy shorts and in-between shorts. This is, and always has been, a personal-choice thing.

If you prefer the freedom of movement that short shorts offer, and you have the legs to pull it off, then by all means opt for short shorts. When it comes to side-split comfort, there's nothing like them.

On the other hand, if you'd rather keep your upper thighs shrouded in mystery—and in nylon/polyester—then, please, go the long-and-loose route. More power to you.

Short shorts do not, by the way, confer any benefits in the speed department. While it's true that most elite runners wear short shorts (or, if they're women, skin-tight "butt huggers"), the act of wearing super-short shorts will not, in itself, make you faster.

RULE 3.5

SAVE THE RACE SHIRT
FOR POSTRACE

WEARING THE OFFICIAL RACE shirt during the race is like wearing a U2 T-shirt to a U2 concert.
Not cool. Don't do it.

RULE 3.6

COTTON SOCKS ARE THE DEVIL

COTTON SHEETS ARE SOFT and lovely. Cotton dress shirts are crisp and smart. Cotton candy is mouthwatering. Cotton socks? None of the above—at least not when you're running any distance to speak of. Doubly so when it's hot and humid and you begin to wonder, about an hour into your sweaty run, whether you need to be in a jungle, per se, to get jungle rot.

When you're running, opt for synthetic or wool socks.

RULE 3.7

WHEN ELASTIC IS GONE,
MAN, IT IS GONE

MEN, THIS ONE IS for you.

You paid good money for those shorts. You love those shorts. You have worn those shorts in the heat and the cold, sun and rain, over hill and dale. You've raced in those shorts—maybe even set a personal record in them.

But, my brother, listen carefully: Sooner or later, there will come a day when you pull those shorts on and feel roomy gaping where once there was a snug liner. This means that the elastic down there has gone slack.

You will be tempted to shrug this off and wear them running anyway.

Don't. Trust us on this one.

You know what? Let's just move on.

RULE 3.8

KNOW WHEN AND WHERE IT'S
OKAY TO WEAR RUNNING APPAREL

ALWAYS
- [ ] During a run or race
- [ ] At a race expo
- [ ] Milling around at the gym
- [ ] In a running store
- [ ] Before, during, or after a sports massage
- [ ] In bed (to save precious seconds the next morning, before an early run)

NEVER
- [ ] In church
- [ ] At weddings
- [ ] At funerals
- [ ] At court appearances
- [ ] At chamber music recitals
- [ ] For job interviews
- [ ] In a rowboat (don't ask why; it would just be weird)

SOMETIMES
- [ ] In hotel lobbies (before or after a run)
- [ ] At work (if you are an elite runner or personal trainer, or if you work at *Runner's World*)
- [ ] At picnics (if you have to run to the picnic or plan to run from it, or if other picnic-goers are also wearing running apparel)
- [ ] At the supermarket (depending on amount of sweat and/or aroma you've generated)
- [ ] On a date (if your date is also a runner, and the two of you are running, have run, or are about to run)

RULE 3.9

DIVERSIFY YOUR WARDROBE

IF YOU HEAD OUT for a run and notice that your cap, shirt, watch, shorts, socks, and shoes are all from the same manufacturer, head right back in and change at least one of the above.

Well, unless you're an elite. In that case, you're all good.

Wearing one brand of gear and apparel from head to toe is okay if you happen to be sponsored by, or are the CEO of, the manufacturer in question. Otherwise, you're kind of inviting good-natured ribbing, at best, and flat-out ridicule at worst. It's like pulling the lever of a slot machine and coming up all NIKE or ADIDAS or MIZUNO. Except instead of a jackpot, you win smirks from onlookers.

I used to see a guy running in Central Park, years ago. Invariably, he was wearing Fila stuff—and only Fila stuff. (He also was a dead ringer for Wayne Coyne of the Flaming Lips, but I digress.) He seemed like a perfectly nice guy, and I'm sure he was. But man, did he look odd. And he wasn't even that fast!

If you don't mind ridicule, by all means, wear the matching stuff. Otherwise, mix it up. For your own good.

RULE 3.10

A CAP WITH A BILL CAN BE YOUR BEST FRIEND

FROM A RUNNING-GEAR-AND-APPAREL PERSPECTIVE, it's hard to imagine a smarter or more versatile investment than a billed cap. Whether it's cotton or synthetic or whatever, a billed cap can keep the sun off your face, or snow or driving rain out of your eyes. Wake up late for a group run (or, heck, a dentist appointment), and it can disguise bed head. More than once, I've stashed energy gels under my hat, during races and long runs. Works like a charm.

If you happen to be an urban runner, you can even use a cap to flag down a taxi.

Buy several, preferably with the *Runner's World* logo.

RULE 3.11

YOU CAN ALWAYS TAKE
OFF CLOTHING

ERR ON THE SIDE of wearing too much.
Well, not *too* too much. You don't want to start a long run wearing shorts, pants, base layer, technical tee, vest, jackets, glove liners, mittens, and wool hat. Especially if it's August.

But it's always easier to remove a layer than it is to add one, particularly if you're 9 miles from home. So plan for this. Dress just a bit warmer than you think you need to. Then be prepared to deal with clothing you've just peeled off en route: "Can I tuck this hat into a waistband? Can I tie this jacket around my waist?" And so on.

RULE 3.12

JUDGE NOT THE RUNNER
IN THE COTTON T-SHIRT

BACK IN THE DAY, according to ancient cave paintings, runners wore cotton shirts.

Some of them even enjoyed running in cotton shirts. Strange, but true.

Fast-forward a few decades, and today we have "technical" shirts, designed to wick moisture away from the skin, keeping you drier and more comfortable. Technical shirts have the added benefit of looking cool, like something astronauts might wear while relaxing, after hours, with a freeze-dried gin and tonic.

Yes, everyone loves tech shirts.

Still, you will encounter the occasional oddball old-timer who runs in cotton (usually cotton race T-shirts, though even those are becoming rare). Treat him with the respect he deserves—for two reasons, at least.

1. Chances are good that he has been running a lot longer than you have, and even if he's not faster than you today, he probably was at some point.

2. Deriding another runner based on what that runner is wearing is just lame. Such an attitude says a lot more about the derider than it does about the one being derided. And what it says isn't pretty.

Besides, someday—if you're very lucky—you might be an oddball old-timer yourself. And how will you feel if someone sneers at you and your old, outdated tech shirts?

RULE 3.13

WHEN IN DOUBT, WEAR GLOVES
AND A HAT

I S IT COLD OUT? Wear gloves and a hat.

Is it just chilly? Wear gloves and a hat.

I guarantee you: You will never regret wearing gloves and a hat. Ever. And eventually, you will regret not having them.

Just wear 'em.

RULE 3.14

WHEN IN DOUBT,
OPT FOR PANTS, NOT TIGHTS

TIGHTS ARE FUNNY THINGS. Not everyone can pull off tights. For starters, there are the superhero jokes. Then there are the obvious anatomical issues. Let's face it: Not every body type is cut out for body-hugging garments. And, for men especially, wearing tights can be a bit too . . . revealing.

All that said, tights can be very satisfying. They hug your body in a very "second skin" sort of way, compress your muscles, and can show off whatever lean mass you've managed to build up.

On the wrong runner, however, tights can be a train wreck.

Rule of thumb: If you're asking yourself whether you should wear tights . . . you probably should not.

SNAPPY RETORTS TO 5 COMMON HECKLES

HECKLE: "Run, Forrest, run!"

RESPONSE: Approach hecklers. In deadpan delivery, recite another Forrest Gump line, such as "I'm not a smart man. But I know what love is." *[Important: Do not blink.]* Repeat as needed until hecklers become uncomfortable and walk away. If time allows, follow them and repeat lines from other Tom Hanks films.

HECKLE: "Woo woo! Nice legs!"

RESPONSE: "At least I have legs." *[Note: This response works only when dealing with a legless heckler.]*

(continued)

HECKLE: "Nice shorts!"

RESPONSE: Assume that this is a sincere compliment, and say something kind in return. For instance, "Woo woo! Nice legs!"

HECKLE: "Faster! Faster!"

RESPONSE: Pause to explain to the hecklers that you would run faster, except that you have a 6-mile tempo run on tap for Thursday, at 10-K pace, and Wednesday is a cross-training day, so today you're just logging an easy 4 or so, and besides, you're still kinda recovering from your long run on Sunday, which was supposed to be 12 miles but you ran 14 to help make up for the fact that you missed the previous Sunday's long run altogether and you were feeling guilty. If the hecklers are still around at that point, try explaining what fartlek is.

HECKLE: "Get off the road!"

RESPONSE: Confound the heckler by replying in French—e.g., "Je ne parle pas Anglais." If the heckler retorts in French himself, you have met your match. Best to get off the road.

The Runner's Rules of Thumb

1. If you see a porta potty with no line, use it. Even if you don't need to.

2. If you have to ask yourself, *Does this driver see me?* The answer is no.

3. If you have to ask yourself, *Are these shorts too short?* The answer is yes.

4. When packing for a race: If you ask yourself, *Will I need this?* the answer is yes.

5. When running in winter: If it's shiny, it's slippery.

6. If the person on the next treadmill can identify the music on your iPod, the volume is too high.

7. For an estimated marathon finish time, double your half-marathon time and add 10 minutes.

8. Never take a cup from the first fluids table.

9. When running in winter: If you're warm before you begin running, you're overdressed.

10. Err on the side of too much massage.

11. 1 glazed doughnut = 2 miles

12. When tapering before a race, don't stand when you can sit; don't sit when you can lie down.

13. Drink when you're thirsty.

14. If you vomit at the finish line, you kicked too hard. Or just hard enough.

15. The more expensive the car, the less likely it is to move over for you.

16. All other things being equal, treadmill is easier than road.

17. Whenever possible, begin an out-and-back run into the wind.

18. Try to eat some carbs and protein within an hour postrun.

19. If you can't maintain a conversation during an "easy" run, slow down.

20. In the real world, cars have the right of way.

21. You almost never regret the runs you do; you almost always regret the runs you skip.

22. Sick? If symptoms are above the neck, you can still run.

23. If you can remove your running shoes while they're tied, they are not tied tightly enough.
24. Recover 1 day for every mile in the race you've just finished.
25. If both your feet are off the ground simultaneously, you are running.
26. Stretch after your run—not before.
27. Not everyone who looks fast really is, and not everyone who looks slow really is.
28. Buying a piece of running gear just because it's on sale is always a bad idea.
29. Buzzing your hair with clippers before a race will make you feel 8 percent faster.
30. Watching a marathon in person is the easiest way to motivate yourself to sign up for a marathon.
31. A long-sleeved shirt and shorts will always look better than a short-sleeved shirt with tights.
32. Owning your own timing chip is like carrying your own pool cue into a bar.
33. If an injury is bad enough to keep you from running properly, it's bad enough to keep you from running, period.
34. You can never have too many safety pins in or on your gym bag.
35. Increase your mileage no more than 10 percent per week.
36. For winter runs, a man never regrets opting for wind briefs.
37. No one sleeps well the night before a race; the night *before* the night before your race is the important one.
38. The first runner to crest a hill is the strongest runner of the group.
39. The last runner to crest a hill is the funniest of the group.
40. Don't wear racing flats unless you can back' em up.
41. If you "need" music in order to run, you're kind of missing the point.
42. On a long run, it's always better to have a bit of toilet paper and not need it, than vice versa.

43. Wearing a terrycloth headband ironically is more annoying than wearing one in earnest.

44. To help keep your upper body relaxed during a run, imagine you're carrying a potato chip in each hand.

45. If you wear it running, keep it out of the clothes dryer.

46. The shorter the race, the more important the warmup.

47. If a road is busy enough to make you wonder if runners are "allowed" on it, avoid running on that road.

48. Two types of runners raise their arms in triumph at the finish line: the runner who has just won the race, and any runner who wasn't even close to winning.

49. Nobody has ever watched *Chariots of Fire* from beginning to end. Not even the people who made it.

50. When the announcer says a race is "tactical," he means "slow."

51. If you care even a little bit about being called a jogger versus a runner . . . you're a runner.

52. Women who race in full makeup are never fast.

53. Women who race in full makeup don't care that they're not fast.

54. The best time of day to run is the time you're most likely to actually do it.

55. Whenever possible, choose a primary care physician who is also a runner.

56. You can't go wrong with Fig Newtons.

57. Shop for running shoes late in the day, not in the morning. (Your feet swell as the day progresses.)

58. A sock makes better TP than a leaf does.

59. If the shorts have a liner, underwear is redundant.

60. If you can't live without it, don't leave it in a gear-check bag.

61. If you can't race without it, don't put it in your checked luggage.

62. At a fluids station, always try to make eye contact with the person whose cup you want.

63. Shin discomfort while running is okay; while walking, not okay. See a doc in that case.

64. You lose fitness faster than you gain it.
65. If you never have a "bad" day, you're probably doing something wrong; if you never have a "good" day; you're definitely doing something wrong.
66. If you're going easy, really go easy; if you're going hard, really go hard.
67. The faster you run uphill, the steeper it seems.
68. Running any given route in the rain makes you feel 50 percent more hard-core than covering the same route on a sunny day.
69. The more often you check your watch, the longer the run will drag on.
70. Every rule of thumb has an exception—except for this one.

RESOURCES

A HANDY REFERENCE GUIDE for runners, including charts, lists, measures, an A-to-Z glossary of running and racing terms, and a little something we call the Pee Matrix.

THE 14 TYPES OF RUNNERS

NAME	DISTINGUISHING CHARACTERISTICS
The Speed Freak	Buzzed hair. Supershort shorts. Racing flats. Twitch in one eye.
The Weekend Warrior	Tube socks. Midsection paunch. Grin. Headphones.
The Penguin	Plodding determination. Fanny pack.
The Charity Runner	Selflessness. Tears. Matching outfits
The Ultra Guy	Lean and tan to the nth degree. Quiet. Hard as nails.
The Baggy Shorts Kid	Youth. Awkwardness. Baggy, possibly knee-length shorts.
The Moaner	Random, intermittent, loud moaning.
The Kicker	None whatsoever . . . until he or she unleashes a stiff, tight-lipped, arm-pumping sprint in the final 100 meters of the race.
The Old-Timer	Faded cotton T-shirt from the 1981 Peachtree 10-K. Scar on neck from melanoma. Twinkle in eye. Conspicuous lack of gadgets. Advanced age.
The Triathlete	Ironman tattoo. Skin-tight unitard, possibly emblazoned with sponsors' names. Comparatively large upper body. Vague smell of chlorine.
The Matching Guy	Every piece of apparel and gear he's wearing is made by the same manufacturer. Every piece.
The Guy You Saw at the Expo	Hey! You totally saw that guy at the expo yesterday!
The Wacky Guy (costumed or otherwise)	"Antennas" headband, oversize novelty sunglasses, cowboy hat, kilt, superhero costume, etc. A grim determination to "have fun with it."
Joe Average	None.

DANGEROUS?
Only if you get in his way
Only if you make fun of his socks.
Only if you make fun of John Bingham.
No . . . unless you are anti-"awareness."
Only if you are an all-you-can-eat brunch buffet.
No, but he will probably beat your sorry butt without breaking a sweat.
Do you really want to get close enough to find out?
Lord help you if you get in the way of those pumping arms.
Heck, no. These guys are great.
Only if you call him a unitard.
No. Just mildly . . . odd.
No. Unless he also happens to be a Kicker.
Probably not, although you're always slightly worried that this guy might snap.
Almost certainly.

THE
BAGGY SHORTS KID

THE PEE MATRIX

WHERE IT'S OKAY TO GO, AND WHEN . . . DEPENDING ON URGENCY AND POPULATION DENSITY

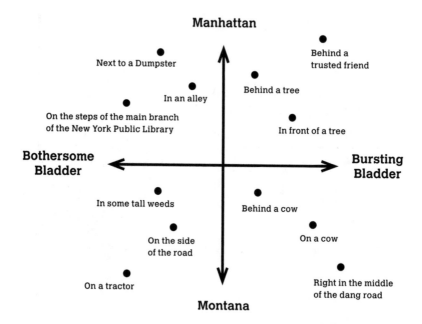

RUNNING BRANDS: A GUIDE TO PRONUNCIATION

Brand	Rhymes with . . .
Adidas	uh, Cletus
Asics	bay six
Etonic	prephonic
Fila	deal a
Karhu	star who
Mizuno	Ms. Juneau
New Balance	new balance
Nike	crikey
Pearl Izumi	Earl is roomy
Polar	so far
Puma	looma
Salomon	Paula Min
Saucony	rockin' knee
Suunto	moon toe

5 TOPICS GUARANTEED
TO GET A RUNNER'S DANDER UP

1. Walking in Marathons: Good or Bad?
2. Running with Headphones: Good or Bad?
3. Dean Karnazes: Good or Bad?
4. Barefoot Running: Good or Bad?
5. Charity Runners: Good or Bad?

5 TIMES IT'S OKAY
FOR A RUNNER TO CRY

1. Finishing your first marathon
2. Finishing your first Boston
3. Qualifying for your first Boston
4. Just missing qualifying for your first Boston
5. During deep-tissue massage

5 BEST SONGS WITH SOME FORM
OF *RUN* IN THE TITLE

1. "Born to Run," Bruce Springsteen
2. "I Ran," Flock of Seagulls
3. "Runnin' with the Devil," Van Halen
4. "Run Like Hell," Pink Floyd
5. "Running to Stand Still," U2

HAND SIGNALS

Motorists usually can't hear you. If you want to get a message across, you'll need to use your hands.

The Polite Forward-Facing Palm = "Hello." / "Thank you for slowing and/or giving me wide berth." / "I come in peace."

The Downturned Palm = "Hey bud, the speed limit here is 35 mph."

The Downturned Palm, Pumped Up and Down = "Perhaps you didn't hear me; I said the speed limit is 35 mph."

The Dual Upturned Palms and Shrug = "I also witnessed that clueless driver and am at a loss to explain his or her behavior."

The V Sign, aka the Peace Sign = "Hello, fellow active-outdoors type."*

Now, we know what you're thinking. We're missing the most popular "hand signal" of all among runners; the upraised-single-digit one. Indeed, no guide to hand signals would be complete without it. And so, without further ado . . .

The Thumbs-Up = "Hey, friend . . . nice driving. Keep it up!"

*Flashed upon noting a roof rack, "26.2" bumper sticker, driver wearing Oakleys, or any combination; or upon having a driver flash you this sign, or a raised fist, first.

THE RUNNER'S GLOSSARY

Some common running terms and how to use them properly.

aid station (n.)

In road racing, a designated point along the course that offers water and (often) sports drinks to competitors, typically handed out by volunteers. Gels, energy bars, petroleum jelly, and other items may be offered as well. Also called *fluid station, water station, or water stop.*

e.g.,

CORRECT: "The aid station at mile 15 offers energy gels, in addition to water and sports drink."

INCORRECT: "If you want to apply for financial aid, station yourself over there and fill out these forms."

bandit (n., v.)

One who participates in a race unofficially, without having registered and paid for it. Also: the act of running a race as a bandit. Also called *jerk.*

e.g.,

CORRECT: "Because he couldn't seem to scrape together the $5 entry fee, Henry ran the Podunk Lions Club 5-K as a bandit."

INCORRECT: "I was looking forward to trying that new sports drink made with absinthe, but they bandit."

bib (n.)

Shorthand for "bib number," the paper or Tyvek sheets printed with a unique number (and sometimes a runner's name) to identify a runner during a race.

e.g.,

CORRECT: "After I check into the hotel, I'm going to the expo to pick up my bib."

INCORRECT: "I loved *Bib.* Especially that scene in the toy store where Tom Hanks plays 'Chopsticks' on that giant keyboard."

chip (n.)

A small plastic disc affixed to the shoelace, used to track a runner's progress and record his or her times during a race. Chips are detected when they pass over an electronic mat at the start and finish of a race course, and often at various points in between. Also called *timing chip.*

e.g.,

CORRECT: "I think I'll put my chip on my shoe tonight, so I don't have to worry about it tomorrow morning before the race."

INCORRECT: "If we all chip in, maybe we can afford a single entry to the New York City Marathon."

chute (n.)

In racing, the area immediately past the finish line. So-called because it is typically long and narrow, meant to keep competitors moving postrace and funnel them away from the finish area.

e.g.,

CORRECT: "After you finish, please continue along through the chute to collect your medal and space blanket."

INCORRECT: "When I told Dan the joke about the race director and the farmer's daughter, it made him chute Fierce Melon Gatorade out of his nostrils."

cooldown (n.) / cool down (v.)

A period of light physical activity, such as jogging, done after a longer and/or harder period of activity. Also: the act of cooling down in such a manner. (*See also* warmup)

e.g.,

CORRECT: "When you finish your final 800-meter interval, do a 2-mile cooldown."

INCORRECT: "Dude, cool down! I'm sorry I called you a jogger!"

corral (n.)

A partitioned area at the start of a race, generally used to group competitors according to projected finishing time, with the fastest runners in the first corral and the slowest in the last.

e.g.,

CORRECT: "My qualifying time for Boston was fast enough to put me in the second corral!"

INCORRECT: "I heard they plan to sink that statue of Paul Revere in the ocean to form a corral reef."

expo (n.)

Short for *exposition,* an assemblage of commercial booths, displays, and (sometimes) informational seminars held in conjunction with a road race, usually in a large hall or convention center. Bib numbers, timing chips, and race packets are typically picked up at a race expo.

e.g.,

CORRECT: "I got some new shorts and a bunch of free energy bar samples at the expo."

INCORRECT: "I'm afraid these new shorts expo's some bits that really should be covered up."

fartlek (n.)

A Swedish word meaning, literally, "speed play." Any run or segment of a run in which pace or effort varies at the runner's whim.

e.g.,

CORRECT: "Instead of my usual speed workout on the track this week, I did a few miles of fartlek on the roads."

INCORRECT: "Cyril was choking on a piece of hard candy, so I performed the fartlek maneuver, and out it came."

flats (n.)

Very lightweight running shoes, minimally constructed with very little support or cushioning, used for racing or for track workouts.

e.g.,

CORRECT: "My new flats make me look fast standing still. I'm going to wear them in next weekend's 5-K."

INCORRECT: "I've been looking at flats all day, mate, and I'm knackered. Let's go round the pub for a pint and watch football on the telly."

fluid(s) station (n.)

(*See* aid station)

interval (n.)

A segment—defined by time or, more often, distance—within a speed or track workout. Speed intervals are interspersed with periods of recovery. Also called *repeat.*

e.g.,

CORRECT: "Today's workout is eight 400-meter intervals with a 200-meter jog in between."

INCORRECT: "Today's forecast: highs in the 70s with intervals of sunshine."

jog (v., n.)

The act of running at a slow, leisurely rate. Also: such a run. Sometimes used, or taken, in a derogatory fashion.

e.g.,

CORRECT: "As a warmup before our speedwork, let's jog a mile or so."

INCORRECT: "If you're going to the supermarket, pick me up a jog of sweet tea."

jogger (n.)

One who jogs. Often disparaging, when directed toward someone who actually cares about that sort of thing.

e.g.,

CORRECT: "Did you see how slow that jogger was moving? No? Well, have another look. Because he's still pretty much in the same spot. That's how slow this guy is."

INCORRECT: "Try hypnosis. Maybe that'll jogger memory."

junk miles (n.)

Any amount of running done at relatively low effort without a particular purpose. Contrast with "tempo run," "speedwork," "fartlek," "long run," etc. Usually derogatory.

e.g.,

CORRECT: "She runs 5 days a week, but it's mostly junk miles."

INCORRECT: "Catalogs, credit card offers, sweepstakes . . . this is all junk mile, y'all."

kick (v., n.)

The act of dramatically increasing one's speed during a race, usually in the final stretch, and usually to beat an opponent or opponents to the finish line. Also: such an effort.

e.g.,

CORRECT: "Thanks to some superhard track workouts, my finishing kick was enough to move up from 478th place to 473rd."

INCORRECT: "I really got a kick out of seeing that guy sprint to beat the runner wearing the tutu."

long run (n.)

Any run that is significantly longer than usual, done at a comfortable, steady pace, with the intention of building stamina. Most training plans call for one long run per week, typically on a Saturday or Sunday.

e.g.,

CORRECT: "I did my long run yesterday, so today I'm going to cross-train."

INCORRECT: "In the long run, we are all adrift in a sea of meaninglessness. So I'm going to skip my workout and sit here reading Kierkegaard instead."

negative split (v., n.)

To run the second half of a run or race faster than the first half. Also: such a performance.

e.g.,

CORRECT: "I totally negative-split that 10-K; I ran the first half in 20:35 and the second half in 19:40."

INCORRECT: "I was trying a new stretch the other day and negative-split my shorts."

pronation (n.) / pronate (v.)

pronation: the extent to which the foot rolls inward.

pronate: the act of pronation.

(*See also* supination)

e.g.,

CORRECT: "My doctor says I overpronate, so I should wear a motion-control shoe to compensate for that."

INCORRECT: "I am so pro-nation, I taught my dog to bark 'Stars and Stripes Forever.'"

rabbit (n.)

A pacesetter, often paid, enlisted to take the leaders of a race through a predetermined distance at a predetermined pace, then to relinquish the lead.

e.g.,

CORRECT: "I heard that marathon hired a rabbit to pace the leaders through the halfway point in 1:05."

INCORRECT: "Sharon is a rabbit Boston Marathon fan; she has every race program ever printed, and named her first child Hopkinton."

repeat (n.)

(*See* interval)

singlet (n.)

A sleeveless, scooped-neck shirt designed for running, typically of synthetic materials. Sometimes called, inaccurately, a tank top.

e.g.,

CORRECT: "Do you think it's warm enough to race in just a singlet? Or should I wear a long-sleeved shirt?"

INCORRECT: "We would love twins but would be just as happy with a singlet. As long as it's healthy."

speedwork (n.)

Any running workout that involves running certain predefined segments at a faster-than-normal pace, interspersed with periods of recovery. Typically done in between a warmup and a cooldown. Also called *intervals* or *track workout*.

e.g.,

CORRECT: "My 5-K time has dropped significantly since I added speedwork to my weekly training schedule."

INCORRECT: "Doc, I'd like to improve my 5-K time this year, pharmaceutically. Will speedwork?"

split (n.)

The time recorded for any specific segment of a run, race, or workout.

e.g.,

CORRECT: "My splits for the Rosie Ruiz 5-K were 8:33, 8:27, and 1:34."

INCORRECT: "Dude, I think the race director knows we cheated. Let's split."

supination (n.) / supinate (v.)

supination: the extent to which the foot rolls outward.

supinate: the act of supination.

(*See also* pronation)

e.g.,

CORRECT: "My doctor said I supinate, so I should wear a stability shoe to compensate for that."

INCORRECT: "My doctor said, 'You supinate,' so I thanked him and said he was super, too."

tempo run (n.)

A training run of a specified duration or distance, done at a steady effort level typically somewhere around 10-K race pace—hard, but manageable.

e.g.,

CORRECT: "I prefer a good 4-mile tempo run to a boring set of intervals on the track."

INCORRECT: "Hey, we're almost out of tempo—I'm going to make a tempo run."

timing chip (n.)

(*See* chip)

track workout (n.)

(*See* speedwork)

treadmill (n.)

A primitive torture device first imagined by medieval jailers and perfected in the late 20th century, designed to destroy one's mind through sensory deprivation and monotony.

e.g.,

CORRECT: "I would rather die of hypothermia than run on a treadmill."

INCORRECT: "Treadmills aren't so bad."

VO₂ max (n.)

The maximum amount of oxygen your body can process.

e.g.,

CORRECT: "I heard that Ryan Hall's VO_2 max is off the charts."

INCORRECT: "I'm looking for shampoo for my wife; I think it's called . . . VO_2 Max?"

wall (n.)

Usually "the wall." The point in a longer race where a runner's energy levels suddenly and catastrophically plummet, leaving the runner feeling as if he or she has hit a literal wall. In a marathon, this typically occurs around miles 18 through 22.

e.g.,

CORRECT: "I felt great through mile 19, then—bam!—I hit the wall hard."

INCORRECT: "*The Wall* is okay, but I prefer *Dark Side of the Moon*."

warmup (n.) / warm up (v.)

A period of light physical activity, such as jogging, done before a longer and/or harder period of activity. Also: the act of warming up in such a manner.

(*See also* cooldown)

e.g.,

CORRECT: "Let's warm up with an easy mile on the track."

INCORRECT: "Is it warm up there? If so, let me know, and I can turn on the AC."

BONUS: WALLET-CARD VERSION OF *THE RUNNER'S RULE BOOK!*

RULES FOR RUNNERS

1. Have fun.

2. Be kind.

3. Start slowly.

4. Run against traffic, mostly.

5. Look before you blow.